# OUT ON HOLY GROUND

# OUT ON HOLY GROUND

## MEDITATIONS ON GAY MEN'S SPIRITUALITY

Donald L. Boisvert

The Pilgrim Press
Cleveland, Ohio

The Pilgrim Press, Cleveland, Ohio 44115
© 2000 by Donald L. Boisvert

Grateful acknowledgment for use of the following excerpted material: "The Way of Some Flesh" by Frank Browning, from *Wrestling with the Angel* by Brian Bouldrey, editor. Copyright © 1995 by Brian Bouldrey. Used by permission of Putnam Berkeley, a division of Penguin Putnam Inc. • From Richard Rambuss, *Closet Devotions* (Durham, N.C.: Duke University Press, 1998). Copyright 1998 by Duke University Press. Reprinted by permission. • From Ronald E. Long, "The Sacrality of Male Beauty and Homosex: A Neglected Factor in the Understanding of Contemporary Gay Reality," in *Que(e)rying Religion: A Critical Anthology*, ed. Gary David Comstock and Susan E. Henking (New York: Continuum, 1997). Reprinted by permission. • From *Love Undetectable* by Andrew Sullivan. Copyright © 1998 by Andrew Sullivan. Reprinted by permission of Alfred A. Knopf Inc. • From Eleanor Brown, "Queer Fear," *The Globe and Mail*, 24 October 1998. Reprinted by permission. • From Donald L. Boisvert, "Queering the Sacred: Discourses of Gay Male Spiritual Writing," *Theology & Sexuality*, no. 10 (March 1999). Reprinted by permission. • From Susan Palmer, *AIDS as an Apocalyptic Metaphor in North America* (Toronto: University of Toronto Press, 1997). Reprinted by permission. • From Frederick Bird, "The Nature and Function of Ritual Forms: A Sociological Discussion," in *Studies in Religion/Sciences religieuses* 9, no. 4 (fall 1980): 393. Reprinted by permission. • From Nancy L. Wilson, "Fear of Faith (a Curable Condition of Gay Men and Lesbians)," *The Harvard Gay & Lesbian Review* 3, no. 4 (fall 1996): 18. Reprinted by permission. • From Tim McFeeley, "Coming Out as Spiritual Revelation," *The Harvard Gay & Lesbian Review* 3, no. 4 (fall 1996): 11. Reprinted by permission. • Material from the Harmonists of Christiansbrunn Brotherhood reprinted by permission. • From *Freedom, Glorious Freedom* by John J. McNeill. Copyright © 1995 by John J. McNeill. Reprinted by permission of Beacon Press, Boston. • By Yukio Mishima, from *Confessions of a Mask*. Copyright © 1958 by New Directions Publishing Corp. Reprinted by permission of New Directions Publishing Corp. • From Paul J. Gorrell, "Circuit Parties as Spiritual Phenomenon," paper presented at American Academy of Religion annual meeting, Orlando, Florida, November 21, 1998. Reprinted by permission. • From Geoff Mains, "Urban Aboriginals and Celebration of Leather Magic," in *Gay Spirit: Myth and Meaning*, ed. Mark Thompson (New York: St. Martin's Press, 1987). Reprinted by permission of Gay Sunshine Press.

We have made every effort to trace copyrights of materials included in this publication. If any copyrighted material has nevertheless been included without permission and due acknowledgment, proper credit will be inserted in future printings after receipt of notice.

Printed in the United States of America on acid-free paper

05  04  03  02  01  00     5  4  3  2  1

Library of Congress Cataloging-in-Publication Data

Boisvert, Donald L., 1951–
    Out on holy ground : meditations on gay men's spirituality / Donald L. Boisvert.
        p. cm.
    Includes bibliographical references (p.   ) and index.
    ISBN 0-8298-1369-1   (paper : alk. paper)
    1. Gay men—Religious life.   I. Title.

BL625.9.G39   B65   2000
291.1'7835766—dc21                                                    99-054448

*Pour Gaston*
*Avec amour*

*Pour mon père*
*Le premier et le dernier*

*For John*
*In friendship*

*For Brandt and David*
*In memoriam*

# Contents

# Preface

THIS BOOK IS ABOUT how we, as gay men, create and inhabit religious spaces. This process I call gay spirituality. As such it is a relatively recent phenomenon, though I would argue, as I do, that the manifestations of our delinquent erotic impulses have always had a spiritual dimension to them. Where we stand today, I suspect, is not fundamentally that much different at heart from where we stood generations ago. We have always used the discourse of the sacred to make sense of our oppression and to validate our identity, regardless of how we may have felt about organized religion as such. Many of us have had to flee the perverse influence of churches, only to find that we had an insatiable urge to reacquaint ourselves with a genuine experience of the holy. In part, these pages explore this phenomenon. They go one significant step further, however. They provide a religious reading of gay lives today, and they argue, in no uncertain terms, that we need to maintain our difference in order to keep making sense of these lives. This book proposes an analysis of the contemporary gay experience from the perspective of the sociology of religion, and even, in some instances, from that of a theology of gay sexuality. It is part personal testament, part prayerful commentary, and part social investigation.

When one writes a book, particularly a first book, questions about its links with the rest of one's life naturally emerge. What does it mean that I am interested in this topic? What specific influences, positive or negative, have brought me to this point? Why write this book, and why at this stage of my life? Such questions, or others like them, help place the book in context. They give it character and soul, shaping it within the contours of the author's life. They also help focus one's energy and enthusiasm, thereby allowing the book to emerge as reflexive and creative activity, as both meditation and manifesto.

As far back as I can recall, religion and male desire have been important to me. I have spent much of my life grappling with each—more successfully, I think, in the case of the latter, less so for the former. My quest for the religious has carried me along some well-traveled and certainly checkered paths. As a child, I wanted to be a priest. My hero was Dominic Savio, a fifteen-year-old Italian saint who was the very model of chastity for young boys. Though perhaps not as valiant as Dominic in defending the purity of my soul (or my body for that matter), I clung as confidently as I could to the rituals and beliefs of my Catholic upbringing. My mother, who died at a young age and who was, I recall, an attractive mixture of piety and sensuality in her daily life, influenced me greatly. She was, and has remained, my muse. Shortly before I entered minor seminary at the age of thirteen, something that she had proudly arranged, she was taken from us by cancer. I left home, literally and figuratively, never to return in any true sense.

My years as a clerical neophyte in the seminary and the novitiate, with a religious community dedicated to the cult of the eucharist, were happy ones. In an atmosphere charged with male presence, I was slowly becoming aware of who and what I was. It was in my novitiate year, only months before taking my initial vows of poverty, chastity, and obedience, that the first real crisis about my sexuality erupted, though I was not fully cognizant of its real meaning until several years later. A close friend, who had entered as a postulant, left, and I was devastated. I had obviously developed a strong attraction to him, and his departure threw into question my sense of self and my vocation. I left in turn.

Upon entering college, I discovered sociology, more particularly the sociology of religion, under the loving tutelage of a young female professor. We developed a close relationship, but separated when, at the age of twenty-two, I fell in love with a man for the first time. I continued my graduate work in religion, eventually completing a doctorate in religious studies. I had, in fact, "intellectualized" my religious impulse. My quest for the sacred had expressed itself in the life of scholarly pursuit. Though I still consider myself a religious person, my spiritual search does not have the magic and wonder of that of the true believer. My grace, I would like to assume, is in teaching and writing about religion, in deciphering its continued relevance for those who, in this day and age, tend to disregard it all too easily.

I have been with my current companion for twenty-three years. It is a loving, comfortable relationship; in many ways, it is the mainspring of my existence. I have also been blessed with very good friends. Some time ago, however, one such friend caused me a great deal of pain by making blatantly homophobic remarks in my presence, and further by dismissing any attempts to discuss the situation. Like most gay men, I have been taunted and teased in my life, and I have experienced subtle but polite forms of discrimination. But this experience made me angry, and that is why I decided, in part, that I needed to write this book. It is my measured but irate response to the arrogance and narrow-mindedness of those who continue to think they can still dismiss us as gay men, thereby undermining the value and meaning of our experience in the world.

This, then, is the ebb and flow of my life; these moments have brought me to this point and to this book. It makes sense that I should write about gay spirituality because it is about religious belief and it is about men. It is about us, as a community and as individuals, trying to come to grips with our demons and with our gods. It is about understanding what makes our lives so precious and meaningful—what makes them truly sacred. Gay theologian Ronald E. Long expresses it thus: "A gay man is one who recognizes and lives by the 'sacrality' of masculine beauty and homosex. And 'coming out' is a gay man's refusal to live a life that belies the sacrality of what he holds sacred."[1] I want this book to be part of my coming out, the occasion for an encounter with what I hold to be precious and sacred in my life.

I offer this book to my gay brothers in the hope that they also will hear the proud echo of their names and their lives in its pages.

Though intensely solitary in effort, a book is never really written in isolation from others. In this, I am grateful to a number of individuals who have made a contribution, whether intentional or not, to the completion of these pages and to the inspiration behind them.

I thank my editor at The Pilgrim Press, Timothy G. Staveteig, for having taken a chance on me. I believe in the power of fate, which managed to bring editor and potential author together. I am grateful for his firm yet gentle guidance, which has undoubtedly brought about a far better book than that springing from my modest attempts and uncertainties as a first-time writer. I also extend gratitude to the managing editor at Pilgrim Press, Ed Huddleston, for keeping everything on track so effortlessly.

To David, who never ceased believing in me and who was supportive to the point of blind enthusiasm, as only friends can be, I extend heartfelt appreciation. He challenged me to see the hand of God in what I was doing, as discouraging as it may have been at times. It kept me going.

I thank the team of Campus Ministry at Concordia University, and particularly the Reverend David Eley, S.J., for giving me an opportunity initially to present some of these ideas in the context of the annual Eric O'Connor lecture.

Parts of the book were given in a preliminary form as papers at academic conferences in Montreal, Amsterdam, and San Francisco. I am grateful to colleagues and friends for their input and commentary.

A very special word of thanks to my lover and life companion, Gaston. He was patient with me and my mood swings, teaching me the tricks of the computer despite my obstinacy, and giving up many weekends doing things together so I could spend my free time writing. I hope he is proud of me, for this book, I would like to believe, is a tribute to the sustaining power of our love.

Finally, to all those men who have entered my life, dark strangers and temporary companions in pleasure, thank you. Your handsome smiles and our passionate flirtations continue to inspire me. I seek and find you anew in every man.

# 1

# A Window on Gay Identity

IN MY DINING ROOM hangs an oil painting by a former fine arts student at the university where I studied and now work. It is a copy of a well-known portrait by Canadian artist Alfred Pellan, entitled *Young Actor*, which hangs in the National Gallery of Canada in Ottawa. The actor is depicted in the costume of a Venetian player, a *saltimbanco*, holding a mask in his left hand and a pipe in his right. However, the fine arts student has painted the word "Queer" in big capital letters boldly across the chest of the seated figure. This simple word radically and dramatically alters our perception of the portrait. It does this by defiantly and unequivocally "naming" what is really present, what we often suspect but do not dare express, or do not want to.

This book is part of that naming. Gay men can truly claim and affirm their lives only by coming out, by naming who and what they are, which includes their experience of the sacred. Gay men's joys and sorrows, their lives and relationships, their amazing ways of celebrating human sexuality and community, and their ways of dying—all require a meaningful interpretive framework, a bigger picture that gives sense and focus to human contingency. The religious is encountered wherever human beings crave and create meaning. All spiritualities, including those we choose to call "gay," are about the carving out of meaning, the bringing forth of transcendence, the ultimate wrestling with the angel, to borrow the title of a bestselling book on the religious experiences of gay men.[1] In the biblical language and imagery of yore, the sacred is encountered and named in this wrestling.

## Spirituality and Society

Spirituality is fashionable nowadays. From excitement over the pastoral visits and moral pronouncements of John Paul II, to the chants and crystals of New Age converts, from the awe and reverence that Mother Teresa still inspires, to the North American fascination with Buddhism, it seems that we have all become believers. If not believers, then we have transformed ourselves into seekers. It is almost as though the ominous approach of the third millennium awakened dormant religious feelings in us, and this significant though artificial date with history forced us to turn, with renewed and fearful fascination, to life's bigger and more compelling questions. Our current search for the spiritual covers a broad spectrum of options, from the traditionally churchy to the outlandishly sectarian, and everything in between. We have so much to choose from that we sometimes lose our way rather than find it.

For the sociologist of religion, such a situation is at once reassuring and unsettling. On the one hand, it confirms the persistence of the religious impulse in human lives, as well as its variety and adaptability. What better argument can there be for the existence of *homo religiosus* than to be able to point to an explosion of spiritual quests at the end of this very secular and barbaric twentieth century? An eloquent case could be made today for the tenaciousness and sheer stubbornness of religion. On the other hand, this revival of belief raises serious and complex questions about the form and shape of religion in today's world, and about the contours of the contemporary religious imagination. What is religious, and what is not? Old definitions are called into question, and very often the so-called religious is found in the most unexpected and exotic places.

This book explores a uniquely postmodern form of religious experience: that of gay male spirituality. In saying this, however, an important and persistent question invariably pops up. Is gay spirituality a *genuine* type of religious expression, or is it another example, albeit more rarefied, of identity politics? Mercifully, the sociologist of religion need not unduly concern himself or herself with the first part of the question. All manner of religious life, by virtue of its creation and living out by human beings, is worthy of respect and investigation. The second part cannot be explained away so easily. It is a significant yet nagging question, for it raises the fundamental issue of the rapport between religion and political culture, and the precise nature of each. It also touches upon some of the more pressing and controversial issues being bandied about in queer theory today. This text cannot avoid grappling with some of these problems and concerns—at times, I hope successfully; at others, undoubtedly less so. I will state at the outset that I believe gay spirituality to be a form of religious expression *and* a manifestation of identity politics. For me, the two are not mutually exclusive.

I wrote this book in response to what I perceived as a twofold need. In recent years, particularly since the onslaught of the AIDS crisis, there has been a rather remarkable outpouring of material, usually in written form, about the religious lives of gay men. This material, as I will discuss later, covers everything from theology to autobiography. Yet in the very midst of such a rich abundance, no systematic effort has been made to assess critically the impact of this material or its meaning as a cultural and sociological phenomenon. Such a lacuna is glaring and unfortunate, for it can only contribute further to misunderstandings about the value and the worth of the gay experience. There is merit in stepping some distance from our lives as gay men, the better to explain ourselves to ourselves and to others.

A second reason for the book has to do with its potential worth as a window on gay lives. The absence of a somewhat more "measured" reflection on the place and the role of religion and spirituality in gay lives, and what the experience means in terms of our identity and the ways, individually or collectively, we choose to express it, is regrettable. We need to make sense of the patterns of our experience—and of their links with the broader culture—the better to appreciate our difference. We also need to cast a sustained and, at times, harsh look at the values, implicit or explicit, that guide and nourish us. This book aims to help us make sense. In a significant way, therefore, it addresses two audiences. The first is gay men everywhere who are struggling with their own religious questions or who want to apprehend the why and wherefore of a key element in the contemporary gay adventure, while the second can perhaps be classified as the more academic or scholarly. Every effort is made to speak to both in a language that will resonate as true and properly nuanced to both sets of ears. I do not wish to claim that this is an unbiased or an "unengaged" book. Because I am a gay man, it could not be otherwise. I can only hope, however, that it does not come across as either naive or unreasonably laudatory. That would be unfortunate, I think.

I am intensely conscious that any study or critical assessment of gay spirituality should not and cannot replace the lived religious experiences of gay men. The sociologist of religion needs to pay close and sustained attention to the shifting patterns of gay lives and to the ways, blatant or hidden, gay men may choose to express their religiosity. Although this work does not attempt to catalog gay men's ways of being religious (others have already done this quite eloquently), it nonetheless builds on their experiences through a process of critical reflection.[2] It can only be hoped that such reflection does not detract from our ability to listen to the rich chorus of gay voices, but adds to their melodic resonance.

This, then, is a sociological study. It is a book *about* gay spirituality. It does not propose any religious paradigms of its own, nor does it delineate any new forms or models of gay spiritual expression. My original title was *Queering the Sacred.* It was a statement about what gay spirituality does. Gay spirituality "queers the sacred." It attempts to circumscribe the holy in terms of the common language and experience of gay men. But a word that is both a noun and an adjective ("queer") was being used as a verb, moreover one in the present tense ("queering"). The implication was clear. This effort at circumscription is ongoing and dynamic; it never really ends; it is always being renewed. Gay spirituality is a continuous search for meaning and relevance—as are all forms of human religious behavior. Gay spirituality is an active, living process, not a moribund set of theological principles. At its most general, therefore, it encompasses the full panoply of ways by which gay men make sense of the religious elements in their lives, the manner in which they reflect upon them and write about them, the myths and stories they recount to remember them, and the structures, symbols, and rituals they create to express them.

## WRITING FROM THE MARGINS

A brief comment on my use of the words "queer" and "gay" may be in order at this point, primarily because readers will note that the former is used sparingly in the text, while the latter is the rule rather than the exception. "Queer" is an old, derogatory word, but one now worn with pride by a younger generation of activist lesbians and gay men. It has several advantages. Apart from being the generally accepted nomenclature at the present time, it denotes defiance in the face of the heterosexual norm. It is also genderless, and therefore much more inclusive of a broader gamut of sexual choices. Since this is a study dealing with gay men, I thought it best to shy away from this particular word as much as possible, precisely because it does not refer exclusively to men. For this methodological reason, I have opted for the traditional and more circumspect "gay." "Queer" is used either because it refers specifically to both gay men and lesbians or because it emerges from and describes particular historical circumstances, notably the late 1980s and after. "Queer," in this context, signifies the rejection of identity politics. It also signifies the transgression of sexual norms, in its most radical sense. It can be seen as a form of political posturing, encompassing and expressing the full gamut of sexual possibilities, from gay and lesbian to bisexual, transsexual, and transgendered persons.[3] In using it, I hint at a broader and more dynamic understanding of the sacred, one that is not limited to, and consequently impoverished by, its all too easy and pervasive identification with the male gender.

In the eyes of some persons, particularly my academic colleagues, my approach to the topic of gay spirituality may appear a bit unconventional. As I indicated earlier, it is obvious that I come to this book as a gay man, and that my perspective and insights naturally reflect this fact. Rather than limit myself to report and analysis, however important and necessary they may be, I also choose to advocate for a gay spirituality. While there can be little doubt that sociological theory informs and sustains my analysis at every level (I would not want it otherwise), readers will pick up on an equally strong desire to affirm and validate gay men's religious experience. My range of sources for this study is broad. It covers the spectrum from scholarly works to casual discussions with friends, and much else in between. Indeed, sometimes simply the fact of my being gay and being part of a unique community with a rather special history provides me with a particular insight. I am intensely conscious that I share a living spiritual tradition calling me to engagement and to witness. My interest, therefore, is much more than an academic one. It emerges from the need to say something about the texture and shape of gay lives—my life—in this day and age. I am also deeply conscious that I disclose much about myself in these pages. I would like to believe that this is the true and necessary condition of any serious theoretical reflection.

I write from the margins. In reflecting on my experience and that of other gay men, particularly in writing about our erotic desires and our sexual practices, I am not engaging in a socially normative process of scholarly analysis, much as my words might be carefully chosen or objectively couched in the language of academe. This book is a deliberate attempt at subversion, a strategic and urgent challenge to heterosexuality and to the power and privilege it claims for itself. If it disturbs, so be it; if it shocks, all the better. Being at the margins is a good and necessary place for a writer. It can be claimed, or one can belong there by force of circumstance. I do both. As a gay man, I have no other space to call my own. As a gay scholar, it is where I choose to stand.

Central to the ideas discussed in this book is an understanding of religion as a significant factor in the emergence and development of personal and social identities. I would argue that the gay identity—and, by extension, gay spirituality—is an eminently social thing. It is created and lived out by human beings in community, and it would be absurd to try to disembody it as a numinous phenomenon existing in some reified cultural space. I make mine the contention of Emile Durkheim, the father of modern sociology, that the social is religious, and the religious is social.[4] From this perspective, the gay experience *in and of itself* can be seen and understood as a form of religious or, at the very least, pseudoreligious discourse. All the more reason why gay spirituality—the ways we construct and declaim our beliefs, myths, and rituals—should be apprehended as something inherently and powerfully social.

Chapter 2 asks the basic question: What is gay spirituality? It offers (1) observations on the unique nature of the gay religious and spiritual experience, including defining parameters for understanding the phenomenon; (2) a summary historical perspective on the development of gay spirituality; (3) a classificatory schema for understanding contemporary gay spiritual writing; and (4) a very brief introduction to key theoretical concepts from sociology and religious studies. As its central theme, chapter 3 posits the existence of a systematic and fairly comprehensive theological worldview—a core of beliefs—embedded in gay spirituality, and it offers a general overview of these main ideas and concepts. The fourth and fifth chapters discuss the myths, symbols, and rituals associated with gay spirituality. Chapter 4 analyzes the paradigms, images, symbols, and stories—the discourse—that anchor and circumscribe the gay spiritual identity. Chapter 5 addresses the place and the role of ritual in gay life, its diversity and its complexity, as well as its reflection in community and its appropriation through sexuality. Chapter 6 deals with the experience of wholeness in gay culture, particularly in reference to the gay community itself as "a site of transcendence." Finally, chapter 7 picks up on a number of the larger questions that have emerged with respect to gay spirituality and gay identity, and it offers reflections for the future.

I cannot claim to speak for my lesbian sisters. I would feel quite inadequate in doing full justice to a discussion of lesbian spirituality, not only because I am a gay man, but also because this spirituality has its own rich roots that are different from those of a gay male spirituality. Others, women mostly, have done outstanding work in this area, and my modest contributions would add little of substance to their trail-blazing accomplishments.[5] I believe, however, that there are many points in common between a lesbian spirituality and a gay spirituality, primarily because, from the vantage point of institutionalized religion, both can be said to be forms of "marginalized" spirituality. This marginality, which reflects the social exclusion caused by sexual desire, gives rise to analogous dynamics of cultural resistance. Though the similarities between both types of spirituality are perhaps not as explicit as might otherwise be desirable in this book, I hope their implicit presence is the occasion for several interesting connections in the minds of readers, both lesbian and gay.

It is customary for writers to assume all responsibility for errors in their texts. I do so willingly. If errors there are, they emerge more from the fact that my reflections may not have been "pushed" far enough rather than from any statistical or factual failing. I can only hope that someone else will come along to subvert and to "push" my work to its ultimate limits. That is the greatest gift any writer or any scholar can possibly wish for.

# 2

# Understanding Gay Spirituality

Sᴇᴠᴇʀᴀʟ ʏᴇᴀʀs ᴀɢᴏ, at the time of the crumbling of the Soviet Union, I recall seeing a wonderful cartoon in a U.S. newspaper that showed a large dinosaur, labeled "Communism," lying on its back with its legs in the air, apparently dead. Standing next to it were three cavemen, two with spears in their hands. The first caveman, with the words "The Right" written on his tunic, is turned to the other, and the bubble over his head reads: "Dinosaur collapsed. No more fun to spear." The second caveman, referring to the third who is standing to the side, responds: "Let's get Og. He's gay."[1]

I was quite taken with this cartoon when I first saw it. It was obviously an intelligent satirical commentary on the need for the political Right to create enemies and monsters to justify its own social and cultural agenda. In this case, the homosexual, the enemy within, assumes the place of communism, the once great and powerful enemy of the cold war, in the political imagination and rhetoric of the Right. Such a process of demonization is not limited to the U.S. context. We can all think of similar examples when this has occurred in history, at times with deadly consequences. This simple cartoon is very powerful in another way. It undermines quite effectively the claims of political legitimacy of the Right and exposes them for what they are. It makes explicit the connection between an ultraconservative ideology and the stereotyping and exclusion upon which it is based,

8

and from which it draws its apparent credibility and strength. The cartoon also speaks of vulnerability. When seemingly mighty and eternal certainties have fallen by the wayside, the groups or individuals most on the margins of society then become the object of fixation and disdain. From excluded, they become disposable.

I thought at the time that the same cartoon could be used to demonstrate the attitude of organized religion toward homosexuality. Rather than being labeled communism, the dinosaur could represent the family. The two cavemen in the forefront are in clerical garb, with crosiers in their hands. One says to the other: "Nuclear family collapsed. What to do?" The response: "It's all Og's fault. He's gay. We burn him." Melodramatic, you may say? Not really, especially when you consider the hatred and extermination to which homosexuals have been subjected throughout history. Though we no longer burn the sodomite and the witch at the stake, gay men and women—whether or not the women are lesbian—continue to be blamed and ostracized for many of society's perceived woes, including the breakdown of that most sacrosanct of all institutions: traditional family life.

Gay men have always had a peculiar love-hate relationship with religion. It is important, therefore, to understand the very intimate connection between the oppression and exclusion of gay men and the emergence of a distinctly gay spirituality. Gays are intensely conscious, personally and collectively, of the disdain in which they have been held by organized religion, most notably Christianity, throughout history. One need only consider in this regard the statements of condemnation that continue to be issued by the Roman Catholic hierarchy.[2] The political and social ostracism of gay men has its source in the oppression of Scripture. The blossoming of a gay spirituality can therefore be seen as a classic example of the positive recuperation, by the victim and the outsider, of the religious discourse of rejection and intolerance—in much the same way that gays and lesbians, for example, may opt to call themselves "faggot," "dyke," or "queer," or wear the pink triangle with pride.[3] In choosing to define themselves as persons with a spiritual life and a language with which to express it, gay men are staking claim to one of the most powerful and persuasive instruments of social, cultural, and political legitimacy, that of religion. In doing so, not only do they attempt to neutralize the sharp sting of religious righteousness, they also create a parallel religious discourse of inclusion and acceptance: sites of defiance and resistance, as it were. Such a parallel discourse, in turn, can become a significant source of personal and collective empowerment. The similarities with the field of liberation theology are striking, and it could be argued that these are more deliberate than accidental. Gay theology came into its own at the same time that several Latin American theologians were confidently redefining traditional Christian teaching with respect to the meaning of human salvation.[4]

Gay spirituality is characterized by a spirit of defiance. In asserting the truth and viability of the gay religious experience, and in creating the conditions that allow it to assume a meaningful and treasured place in the lives of gay men, gay spirituality situates itself squarely in opposition to the orthodox religious norm. Though some forms of gay spiritual life may be very much tied in with more established churches, gay spirituality, as a whole, is transnormative. It may borrow blatantly and deliberately from a universal storeroom of religious symbols and rituals, but it posits a radically different understanding of the human body and of human sexuality, on the one hand, and of human relationships with the holy or with the sacred, on the other. This subversive element—vis-à-vis both the transcendent and the immanent—gives gay spirituality its force and dynamism, and makes it an essential constituent of the contemporary gay identity.

Whenever I have told friends and acquaintances that I was in the process of writing a book on gay spirituality, they have inevitably expressed their reaction in one of three ways. First, there are those who smile rather smugly and then quickly decide that the topic somehow needs to be changed, as though I had disclosed an embarrassing fact about myself. In the second group, which is slightly more polite, are those who do not quite understand why I should be writing about something so specific or so exclusive to one group of people. They will ask, "Why don't you just write about spirituality generally? And by the way, why does there have to be a 'gay' spirituality?" People in the last group, while certainly more encouraging, are more curious than anything else. They just do not know what I am talking about: "What is it?" Three sets of responses, three sets of assumptions. They range from the mildly homophobic to the downright puzzled, yet they have one thing in common: ignorance. People do not comprehend what gay spirituality is or why we may need or want to write about it. Some even go so far as to consider it a passing fad, just another example of the faggots taking up too much place again.

I will admit to a certain measure of ignorance until a few years ago. Like most well-informed gay men, I knew about the existence of the Metropolitan Community Church and I had heard about the Sisters of Perpetual Indulgence and their antics,[5] but I did not have a clear or subtle sense of the complexities of gay men's search for spiritual meaning in their lives. I was well acquainted with the shrill and desperate voices of condemnation and hatred coming from organized religion down through history, yet I did not have an appreciation for alternate forms of the gay religious quest. Then the devastation of AIDS came along, and with it a burgeoning of spiritual questionings and possibilities. Like many others, I decided to listen closely to the angry voices and to the hushed prayers. And what I heard was the loud and persistent echo of gay men, present and past, encountering the sacred and trying to make sense of its earth-shattering presence in their lives. We therefore begin with an apparently simple question: What is gay spirituality?

## DEFINING THE PARAMETERS

Before we can attempt to provide a reasonable answer to this question, we need to consider the meaning of the term "spirituality." In most religious traditions, "spirituality" refers to the unique medium or path by which persons seek to live out their religious beliefs and values, either as individuals or as members of a community, but always within the overall framework of the broader tradition. One example is Franciscan spirituality, which is inspired by the work and creative religious vision of Saint Francis of Assisi, but remains part of the larger Christian tradition. Spirituality is a way of focusing and delineating one's life experience in terms of a unifying religious purpose. It expresses the particular way one relates to the godhead. In Christian spirituality, this relationship can generally be mediated in one of two ways: theologically, via formal dogma and belief; or anthropologically, through interaction with other persons. A third form claims to do away with mediating agencies and espouses the possibility of a direct encounter with the godhead. The two most common examples of this type of spirituality are the New Age movement and the Christian charismatic movement.[6] Today, the term "spirituality" is used increasingly to mark a rejection of organized or institutionalized religion, and to refer to the personal search for religious enlightenment. The cover of a U.S. magazine proclaimed: "Believe it or not: Spirituality is the new religion."[7] Consider also the following words by Nancy Wilson, senior pastor of the gay and lesbian Metropolitan Community Church in Los Angeles:

> "Spirituality" connotes a non-institutional, individualistic belief system, a private path to peace or enlightenment. It has none of the dreadful associations of "religion." Indeed, spirituality is quite popular in our communities nowadays. It is very amenable to a consumer mentality: one can sample, shop, or "surf" for spirituality, which is seen as a harmless activity. Spirituality, in short, is a code word for unorganized, harmless religion.[8]

It is not accidental, I would submit, that the pastor of what may be the world's largest lesbian and gay religious congregation should speak in such terms. It reflects well the kind of eclectic approach taken by several with respect to traditional belief systems in today's world. In a highly rational and bureaucratic world, spirituality, by default, takes on many qualities of what is *not* rational or bureaucratic. It may be "a harmless activity" because it does not require the high level of commitment and discipline that traditional religious adherence does. Some say that spirituality is too facile, demanding neither time nor serious engagement, that its disciples remain content with the superficiality of the old adage "be a good person," all the while expending inordinate amounts of time and money on the egotistical search for inner peace and enlightenment. Is spirituality really only this, a vacuous pursuit of the self? Or is it something more deeply engaging and critical?

For the social scientist, the term "spirituality" remains questionable. This catchall quality makes the word difficult to circumscribe. It therefore needs to be handled with care. Some, such as Canadian scholar of religion William Clossen James, reject the term altogether, preferring the traditional yet more malleable "sacred." James points out that "the word 'spirituality' has problematic overtones, suggesting not only inwardness and private faith, but something not entirely to be taken seriously, perhaps because of the implied association with New Age movements."[9] This observation raises the question of the unmistakable historical link between spirituality and the New Age. There can be little doubt that the emergence of a more personalized, less institutionalized form of religiosity owes much to the widespread influence of New Age beliefs, where spontaneity and personal revelation occupy a prominent place.[10] As James also indicates, further difficulties with the word have to do with its association with individual piety and private forms of devotion, as well as its implied eclecticism with respect to matters of belief and dogma. Personal expressions of religiosity are inherently problematic from the perspective of a theoretical understanding of religious phenomena, precisely because they are so contingent upon the self-definition of the believer. A similar difficulty emerges when considering disparate forms of religious practice that have been fused together.

Despite these methodological difficulties associated with the term "spirituality," the word remains a commonly understood and accepted one. Its inherent contradictions may provide us with the clues necessary to understand its nature. When people remark that they are spiritual persons, or that they have had a spiritual experience, chances are that their listeners will understand them. Quite apart from the explicit content of such an experience, which can always be questioned or even rejected, we accept that it is a legitimate form of human response to an encounter with something "beyond" ourselves. Increasingly, we are prepared to recognize and accept the so-called paranormal as a source of spiritual revelation and insight, as much of popular culture demonstrates so eloquently.[11] Much of the discourse around spirituality today clearly has to do with such old-fashioned concepts as values, ethics, care of the self and of others, meaning, and authenticity. This demonstrates in no uncertain terms that organized religion no longer provides the venue necessary for the fulfillment of these ideals, while also speaking eloquently to their continued relevance and significance in people's lives.

Spirituality can be considered anti-institutional in that it rejects or moves beyond organized religion. Perhaps the simplest way to understand it is that it stands in opposition to both church and sect. When our contemporaries hear the word "religion," they immediately associate it with structure and fixed beliefs, with formal liturgies and churchly obligations. Spirituality is amorphous; it resists formal codification. In this sense it can absorb much while rejecting almost nothing. It is utterly and unabashedly personal. More important, it stands in an antithetical rapport to formal religion, which has assumed, in the lives of many, an irrelevant, almost nefarious role. The contemporary quest for the spiritual, in a word, implies a rejection of religious structure and formalism. Although such a rejection may be another example of the self-centered values of the baby boomer generation, it still implies defiance. This sort of defiance is always best expressed by persons at the social margins because they have experienced rejection by religious institutions in the most intimate and direct ways possible—hence the confident emergence of a feminist spirituality, an African American spirituality, and a gay spirituality, among others.

When speaking of spirituality, we must therefore remember that it can be one of two almost opposing things. Operating within a defined religious tradition, it connotes a path chosen in greater fulfillment of the obligations and tenets of that tradition. In this sense, it can be terribly mainstream and conservative. Spirituality understood in its more contemporary vernacular usage, however, implies the opposite: an attitude inspired and defined by personal revelation and enlightenment, a deliberate move away from the rigid formalism of orthodoxy. As paradoxical as it may seem, people today claim to be spiritual because they do not want to be perceived as unduly religious, almost as if there was shame attached to religious practice itself. Could one call this the revenge of religion in the guise of secularism?

We must consider three significant elements when we look at gay spirituality: (1) its function as critical religious discourse; (2) its role as a form of political analysis and engagement; and (3) its positive relation with respect to human gender and sexuality. Each is linked to the other, while the whole is greater than the sum of its mutual yet disparate parts.

By its very existence, gay spirituality implies a critique of organized or formal religion. In particular, it proclaims the essential goodness and value of homosexuality and the worth of the homosexual person. Gay spirituality is an almost total reversal of traditional Western religious teaching on homosexuality: homosexuality is not a sin; the homosexual is not a condemned person; homosexuals must be accepted as full members of the religious community. Not only does it turn this teaching around; it also puts forward a model of its own. This model speaks of the special grace of being gay, of the salvation that comes from self-acceptance, and of the unique historical role of the gay community. In other words, gay spirituality proposes a parallel or alternative religious discourse, one quite unique and radical in its comprehensiveness. Gay spirituality invents and structures a new universe of meaning.

Of necessity, such a discourse must be founded upon a thorough and far-reaching critique of the scriptural bases of homosexual oppression. Since much of the homophobia of Western culture finds its inspiration and justification in the Judeo-Christian Scriptures, subjecting these Scriptures to a rigorous process of theological deconstruction is quite important. This process properly situates and explains the cultural assumptions of the scriptural writers while it reveals their true intent and highlights the misinterpretations throughout the centuries. In this way, gay spirituality undermines and challenges well-entrenched theological beliefs. It undercuts their credibility and offers a model for understanding traditional religious tenets and their continued relevance today.

Gay spirituality subverts religious language and imagery. For example, gays often refer to themselves as members of a tribe. The image is intentionally apt because it speaks of exclusivity in the anthropological sense and it denotes a chosen status of almost mythical proportions—a statement of defiance in opposition to the normative heterosexual world. In the tradition of the Hebrew Scriptures, "tribe" carries rather powerful religious overtones. The tribe is a group "set apart," chosen for a particular purpose by the Deity, who gives it a clear and securely defined identity, and who makes it part of an overarching plan of salvation. Gay spirituality builds on this imagery in significant ways, largely by reappropriating the term and then by giving it a different political twist.

Gay spirituality, however, is much more than subversive religious discourse. It is also about political analysis and engagement. There can be little doubt that the recent flowering of interest in gay spirituality would not have been possible without a climate of acceptance brought about by the intense political struggles of recent decades. The same could be said, for example, about the emergence and mainstream acceptance of queer literature.[12] As always, the political defiance of gay men—and their many strategic successes in this regard—have empowered them to name their experience "religious." The discourse of gay spirituality has emerged directly from the praxis of gay activism. This activism has been especially prominent in recent years, with the arrival of the AIDS crisis and its resultant devastation.

While this crisis has seen the rise of rather interesting forms of gay activism, it has also witnessed the emergence of a unique type of charitable practice, or spiritual work, among gays. Many agree that the gay community as a whole, by responding the way it did to the AIDS crisis—in essence, by doing what governments, churches, and the health care establishment were too cowardly to do in the early years—has given society an eloquent lesson in old-fashioned Christian charity. For those old enough to recall traditional Catholic teaching with respect to the corporal works of mercy, this will ring very true.[13] Such a lesson has not been limited to caring for the sick and dying, however; it has also been one of anger, of criticizing and confronting the powers that be for failing in their public responsibilities. In such situations the religious and the political intersect, and gay spirituality assumes its full power as a transformative agent. Here again, gay spirituality has given a new twist to some very old-fashioned religious values.

In a discussion of gay spirituality (or any so-called minority or marginal form of religiosity for that matter), the personal is truly the communal or the political, and vice versa. This interdependence needs to be underscored because it is central to the gay experience and identity, including their religious dimensions, since those tumultuous days and nights of Stonewall 1969.[14] One cannot fully understand the contemporary gay sensibility without the gay community *itself* as a reference point, just as one cannot divorce the gay religious experience from the history of gay oppression. Gay spirituality is a deliberately political and politicized act. Through a dual, dynamic process of subversion and affirmation, it creates a new paradigm for gay men. Grounded in the hard political reality of gay exclusion and ostracism, it asserts the positive healing force of the gay spirit. It does this through the medium of what is most problematic and worrisome to organized religion: sexuality and the human body—problematic because it is the source of pleasure, and worrisome because it cannot be controlled.

Needless to say, gay spirituality holds a radically different view of the human body—and consequently of sexuality—from that found in institutionalized religion, particularly the Judeo-Christian tradition. The body as source of pleasure, as prime mediating agent in the structuring of a relation of playfulness with the world, is a recurring and omnipresent theme. The body and sexuality are seen as good things to be enjoyed simply and fully as manifestations of the sacred. What is particularly striking is the complete break that this view effects between sexuality and monogamy, as opposed to the powerful message to the contrary found in most, if not all, religious traditions. This may not be surprising in itself, but it points to a fundamental shift in the theological understanding of the body as the instrument of procreation, essentially because same-sex sexual acts are, by their very nature, nonprocreative. For example, this view constitutes an outright rejection of traditional Catholic teaching with respect to homosexuality and natural law, which argues that an openness to procreation is a *conditio sine qua non* of sexual union and, ultimately, of human love.[15]

A recurring argument is that a distinctively gay or queer contribution to human spirituality might be the way in which it understands and portrays relations with the godhead in erotic terms. The erotic, some have remarked, may indeed be the essential quality and defining feature of same-sex relationships, but there is a sense in which the erotic also provides a meaningful opportunity to encounter the sacred because it is characterized by freedom and vulnerability. It is a gratuitous act. These qualities should also inform and define the human rapport to the divine. To see the godhead as lover—as a source of pleasure—is to enter into a privileged moment with another person, albeit divine, where one stands exposed and naked, ready to be transformed. To pick up on a theme that will be explored later, the erotic, for gay men, implies receptivity and penetration. Appropriately enough, these are classic mystical terms for describing union with the godhead, and they point to key elements that gay spirituality exploits effectively.

Gay spirituality affirms and celebrates human bodies and human sexuality, and it does so precisely because religion has so often condemned and manipulated them. Gay men have long been defined not by who they were, but by the types of sexual acts in which they engaged. Even the labels and names by which they were (and still are) designated—"sodomite," "bugger," "pederast"—carry the dispassionate, cold overtones of clinical scientific discourse, as though neither desire nor pleasure was part of the equation. For many Christians, and even others who consider themselves nonbelievers, however, these are not merely sexological terms, but true sins in the sight of God. Gay spirituality rejects such archaic and tainted notions of sinful acts and a judgmental God. In their stead, it proposes a more creative paradigm centered on acts of sexual freedom and the existence of a nonjudgmental, androgynous godhead. In this paradigm, it is not the gay man who emerges as the sinner, but the unrepentant homophobe.

Gay spirituality uses the language of sexual identity as opposed to that associated exclusively with specific sexual acts. In this sense, gay spirituality exemplifies and confirms the modern idea of "the homosexual" as someone who, quite apart from his proclivity to engage in same-sex acts, carries a unique identity or presence in the world. Several authors have pointed out that homosexuals did not really exist as a social category prior to the emergence of the modern idea of identity.[16] Though historians have argued over the particular cultural or economic circumstances that may have made this possible, they agree that it is, relatively speaking, a fairly recent occurrence in the annals of human history.[17] Having a specific homosexual identity implies that there is "a homosexual way" of being religious. It further implies that this "way" is constitutive of identity, and that one must necessarily be religious in a particular way to be genuinely homosexual. From the perspective of the postmodern gay identity, therefore, gay spirituality is an ontological necessity, just as gay activism, to a certain extent, is.

We return to our initial question: What is gay spirituality? In discussing its characteristics, we have examined how it consists of three elements in symbiosis: critical discourse, political action, and sexual affirmation. Gay spirituality reveals the ways by which gay men define, recognize, and assert themselves, not only as individuals having a religious dimension, but as beings whose very difference is the source of their spiritual and historical election. It can best be understood as something that stands *in opposition to* normative patterns of religious belief and action, though it certainly borrows heavily from them. Gay spirituality might not even be necessary if formal or institutionalized religion were more accepting of homosexuality. By default, therefore, it has stepped into the breach and answered the call to prophecy. From hovering in the wings, it has moved center stage.

## A Sense of History

For ease of understanding, the historical development of gay spirituality, at least in the relatively contemporary period, can be divided into three broad segments: pre-Stonewall, post-Stonewall, and the advent of AIDS and its aftermath. The choice of the Stonewall riots as a divider does not imply that this specific historical event should be understood as an absolute transcultural marker or reference point. Rather, it reflects the unique position of Stonewall as the mythic watershed event of modern gay liberation, certainly in the West.[18] In the words of Annamarie Jagose, author of *Queer Theory:* "Stonewall functions in a symbolic register as a convenient if somewhat spurious marker of an important cultural shift away from assimilationist policies and quietist tactics, a significant if mythological date for the origin of the gay liberation movement."[19] Stonewall therefore serves a dual purpose, both historical and symbolic. On the one hand, it marks a break in time, signifying important political and cultural changes; while on the other, it assumes the role of original myth, the paradigmatic founding event of the contemporary gay consciousness.

If one were asked to name the fathers of gay spirituality in the English-speaking world, the names Edward Carpenter and Walt Whitman would be prominent among them.[20] Contemporaries, these two men—one a social critic and reformer, the other a poet—were instrumental in the elaboration of a novel approach to gay spiritual awareness. Though neither was religious in the strict sense of the term, their writings are strongly infused with images and language that touch upon the cosmic role of homoerotic desire. Both put same-sex male attraction at the very center of their philosophies. Their influence continues to be felt to this day, although they are read less frequently now than they once were.

The outlooks of both men are decidedly spiritual. Carpenter's view of what he calls Uranian love, his understanding of androgyny, and his sense that homosexuals have a very special cultural role to play by virtue of their sexual difference—all this colored by the Hellenic aesthetic of his time— make him a visionary thinker. Gay spiritual activists continue to espouse his ideas today. Whitman's imagery of sweet comrades, of manly democracy and an almost mystical universal brotherhood, of men at war, and of the sacred bonds of male friendship—these themes find an echo in the discourse and rituals associated with the contemporary gay search for spiritual identity and meaning. The visions of both men continue to be formative for gay spirituality, and their powerful insights nourish and sustain it.

It could be argued that gay spirituality in the immediate pre-Stonewall period was more akin to the countercultural beliefs normative in the 1960s and early 1970s. These represented a mixture of such elements as androgyny, American Indian traditions, California-based therapeutic rituals, the New Age, and other similar themes and movements. The gay spirituality of this time was not explicitly or deliberately religious. Rather, it partook of the more general search for a unique form of universal spiritual consciousness that was believed to transcend confining generational and gender-based distinctions. Within this search, the quest for the emancipation of the homosexual was to be one among many forms of human liberation. Even today, this strain of gay spirituality remains very much present and influential, enough to constitute a significant discourse in and of itself. It is not merely coincidental, for example, that the founders of the earliest gay rights organizations should have become heavily involved with groups such as the Radical Faeries. During this period, institutionalized religion was under heavy criticism from gay liberation groups and activists. It was understood and perceived, and rightly so, as only one element in a vast and complex panoply of social and cultural institutions oppressing homosexuals and instilling them with fear and self-loathing. This view of religion continues to be central to gay spirituality, though now it has become considerably less strident.

One figure stands out during this time: Harry Hay.[21] Considered the father of the modern gay liberation movement because he founded the Mattachine Society in 1953, the first national U.S. organization committed to political action on behalf of homosexuals,[22] Hay shared the unique cultural vision of Edward Carpenter. His perception of the special role or calling of gays—as reflected in the existential questions "Who are we?"; "Where have we come from?"; and "What are we here for?"[23]—was central to the elaboration of a spiritual vision of the modern gay experience. The Mattachine Society, despite its inherent problems and its ultimate disintegration, was the locus for interesting attempts at introducing a sense of ritual into gay organizing.[24] Hay was also instrumental in setting up the Radical Faeries in 1979, another group that continues to exert a significant influence on the quest for an authentic gay spirituality.

The post-Stonewall era saw the development of organizations and institutions geared specifically to the religious needs of gay men, thereby marking the true emergence of a gay spirituality in the formal sense of the word. The Metropolitan Community Church,[25] even though it was founded in 1968, and the flourishing of such groups as the Anglican "Integrity" and the Roman Catholic "Dignity," support groups for homosexuals of those particular denominations, are examples. During this period many ground-breaking historical and theological works by gay scholars were published, most notably John McNeill's *The Church and the Homosexual* and John Boswell's *Christianity, Social Tolerance, and Homosexuality*. These works, and a handful of others like them, were instrumental in the development of a uniquely gay perspective on the Christian tradition, particularly in their elaboration of alternative readings of controversial scriptural passages and theological traditions. Though the theme of religious oppression remained foundational, the overall effort during this time focused more on a positive recuperation of organized religion, most

notably through the creation of parallel religious structures and institutions, and on a critical rereading of the Bible in light of the gay experience.[26]

In any discussion of gay spirituality, the Metropolitan Community
Church (MCC), known officially as the Universal Fellowship of Metropolitan Community Churches, occupies a lofty place of honor, both historically and theologically. Founded the year before the Stonewall riots by
the Reverend Troy Perry,[27] a defrocked Pentecostal minister, the MCC
now has some 315 congregations in more than 15 countries. Estimated
membership is more than 50,000. It is the only religious institution in the
world catering specifically to the spiritual needs of gay men and lesbians.
As such, it exerts a great deal of moral authority in the gay community with
respect to all things religious. Its leaders have always advocated a theology
of human sexuality, which is an interesting yet delicate balance of gay-
positive and born-again Christianity.[28] In recent years, the MCC has had
to confront the question of its continued relevance. The Reverend Mel
White, one of its more high-profile ministers, has stated: "For me, one
of the challenges for MCC is to create a community for the new millennium that brings spiritual renewal in the way we brought sexual renewal in
the '70s. We need to bring homo*spirituality* in the way we brought homo-
*sexuality.*"[29]

The AIDS crisis has had the most significant and vigorous effect on the
quest for a gay spirituality, and understandably so. The immediacy and
impact of death as a tragic personal and collective experience, and its dramatic association with the sexual life force, the tearing apart of gay relationships and loves, the naked and terrifying encounter with disease and
degeneration—all invariably bring questions of faith to the fore, as they
have throughout the ages. The period since the mid-1980s has been characterized by an outpouring of books on all aspects of gay spirituality: from
historical-theological justifications for same-sex marriages to collections
of essays on the religious experience of gay men, to say nothing of works
dealing with the moral and ethical dilemmas posed by AIDS.[30] There has
also been a resurgence of interest in the spiritual options offered by the
Eastern traditions, most notably Buddhism.[31]

AIDS has provided gay men with an extensive array of new symbols
and rituals that allow them to make sense of the calamity. It has also given
rise to rather unique forms of spiritual experimentation. Susan Palmer, in

the chapter entitled "Healing Homophobia" from her interesting book *AIDS as an Apocalyptic Metaphor in North America*, surveys some of these original and unusual responses.[32] She also highlights the continued pull that "alternative conceptions of reality"[33] exert on gays searching for acceptance and understanding in the face of homophobia. Specifically, Palmer argues that "gays are frequently enthusiastic participants in new religions that require no more than a loose affiliation from members, make no claims of epistemological exclusivity, and charge fees for training in psychotherapeutic and magical techniques often used for secular ends."[34] Examples include New Age groups, the human potential movement, Wiccan and neopagan covens, and UFO cults.

Palmer draws a perceptive comparison between the feminist movement and the gay movement in terms of the reasons for their respective attempts at "spiritualization":

> The spiritualization of the gay movement is not unlike what happened in the feminist movement in the mid-1970s, when books on the Mother Goddess, ancient matriarchies, witches, and the mystical aspects of natural childbirth began to appear. While one could argue that any major cultural movement, as it broadens and deepens, will very likely undergo a spiritual or psychoanalytical phase (what some historians might trivialize as a "quiescent" phase), it is perhaps not a coincidence that both movements developed spiritual interests during those few years when their participants confronted life's most compelling mysteries. For feminist baby boomers embarking on pregnancies in their late thirties, it was facing the trauma of giving birth. For body-conscious gays in the late 1980s, it was living with a disfiguring and fatal disease.[35]

From this historical overview, it is possible to speak of a "progression" in the quest for a gay spirituality. This quest has moved from an argument centered on why gays should be at the common table to one that explores and envisions their sitting at a completely different table—a table of their own design and choosing.[36] In other words, gay men have reached a level of political maturity and sophistication so that it becomes possible and necessary for them to imagine a spiritual life echoing their own life experience as well as their distinct values and aspirations. Though this table can at times be rather peripheral in terms of the religious mainstream, it is nonetheless a richly laden one.

## CONTEMPORARY GAY SPIRITUAL WRITING

In a discussion of contemporary gay spiritual writing, a rather broad and inclusive approach is essential. I therefore consider as "spiritual" both the gay theological treatise and the gay historical study on religion (as well as pretty much everything in between) because both forms of writing seek to place the gay experience within a legitimate religious and spiritual context. In this sense, they are the building blocks of an authentic and comprehensive gay spiritual heritage. It could be argued that gay spiritual writing emerged from, and is founded upon, gay historical study. The explosion of gay historical writing in recent years is a truly extraordinary phenomenon. It speaks eloquently to the need for sexual minorities to understand their past with critical pride before they can hope to change the conditions of their present marginalization.

Contemporary gay spiritual writing can generally be understood and analyzed in terms of a four-dimensional typology. The four types or modes of discourse are (1) the apologetic, (2) the therapeutic, (3) the ecological, and (4) the autobiographical. Each word is first and foremost descriptive: it refers to the tradition or form of expression from which each type stems, or to which it can lay claim. In another sense, the labels suggest what each type is meant to do or to accomplish. Needless to say, as with all such neatly compartmentalized categories, there is much fluidity among them. And these groupings are not necessarily all-encompassing. Gay spiritual writing could be studied and comprehended from a different paradigmatic perspective.

The first mode of discourse, *the apologetic*, does not imply anything negative. The term is used in its theological sense of "reasoned defense." The apologetic mode of gay spiritual writing refers to the particular form of theological or historical discourse that seeks to interpret, or rather reinterpret, traditionally negative religious teachings on homosexuality—particularly those from the Judeo-Christian tradition—in a more gay-positive fashion. Apologetic discourse is not simply reactive, however. Studies that uncover and reclaim hidden elements of the religious inheritance of the gay community are equally important.[37] What distinguishes the apologetic type from others is the fundamental notion of "defense," that is, the attempt to provide alternate or correct interpretations of the gay experience in the light of religious teaching, and vice versa. Very often, this will take the form of an exegesis of problematic or downright injurious passages from the Hebrew Scriptures and the Christian Scriptures—the famous excerpt from Genesis on the destruction of Sodom and Gomorrah and the teachings of Paul with respect to same-sex couplings perhaps being the best cases in point. Apologists will often try to counterbalance these passages by pointing to more positive excerpts from Scripture dealing with human sexuality, and they will emphasize that Jesus apparently never taught anything with respect to homosexuality.

Other characteristics of the apologetic type include a concern with high standards of academic research and a core belief that religion has been manipulated or used to work against gays and lesbians (thereby adopting what might perhaps be seen as a certain optimism and naïveté vis-à-vis religious tolerance). Though the word "revisionist" is problematic in this context, given that it is such a loaded term, we need to ask ourselves whether this is not also a trait of this form of gay spiritual writing. Among the authors whose writings can be defined as apologetic, John Boswell and John McNeill are preeminent, though the latter also espouses a decidedly therapeutic perspective. Others writing within this tradition are Peter Gomes, Robert Goss, and Mark Jordan.[38]

The apologetic mode of discourse can be considered foundational in terms of the others. Only a rigorous scholarly analysis of gay history, and of the ways in which organized religion and traditional theological discourse have mistreated and marginalized gay men, can provide the groundwork necessary for the elaboration of a genuinely gay spirituality and theology. The other modes—the therapeutic, the ecological, and the autobiographical—must be grounded in the gay experience of history and of its vicissitudes for them to acquire any particular meaning or purpose. As the old ghost of that atheist Karl Marx might put it, the theory stems from the praxis, from lived and, at times, (mis)recorded history.

The second type of writing is *the therapeutic*. It is, in many ways, the most easily understood since it is the closest to the lived experience of gay men. The therapeutic form of gay spiritual writing, as would be expected, seeks to place the individual experience of being gay in a strongly positive, legitimate, celebratory, and psychologically healthy context. It emphasizes the beneficial impact of the coming out process for the person. What the apologetic mode of discourse does for gay men as members of a historical community, the therapeutic does for them as distinct individuals. Its message is unequivocally clear: the godhead created sexuality in its variety of forms, and what is created is good; as a gay person, you are good.

One should not underestimate the power and impact of such a simple message. It addresses—and redresses—the very painful experience of self-hatred and rejection that remains the lot of too many gay men, hence the reason for its strong appeal. Much of therapeutic spiritual writing is concerned with issues of loss and with the recovery that can flow from it. There are many close natural affinities between religion and therapy. Each can function in similar ways at the level of the individual psyche. A spirituality that bridges the two can be quite effective in providing a reassuring sense of wholeness and "redemption" to the injured person. This *salvation motif* is the predominant theme of the therapeutic type of gay spiritual writing. This same message of salvation or redemption echoes forcefully throughout *all* of gay spirituality.

The therapeutic mode of spiritual writing or discourse provides an interesting opportunity and context for the subversion of traditionally negative psychoanalytic views on homosexuality, primarily by means of reappropriation of the language of psychoanalysis. Much of it is decidedly more Jungian than Freudian in its orientation, concerned with universal archetypes and symbols. In this regard, one must acknowledge its ongoing debt to many West Coast–based human potential movements that emerged in the 1970s and continue to exert some measured, though significant, influence. Among those writing in the gay therapeutic tradition are John McNeill, who combines a theological approach with a classic psychoanalytic one, John Fortunato, Craig O'Neill and Kathleen Ritter, and Christian de la Huerta.[39] These authors, and others like them who write or work in the field, are practicing psychoanalysts, psychologists, or counselors, and several of them adopt a classic twelve-step recovery approach to gay spirituality, based on a model borrowed from Alcoholics Anonymous.

*The ecological*, the third type of writing, is perhaps the most all-encompassing. It includes such major thinkers and writers as Harry Hay, Will Roscoe, J. Michael Clark, Daniel Spencer, and Ronald Long.[40] The three most striking features of the ecological form of gay spirituality are its strong theological flavor, its eclecticism, and its ecological imagery and discourse. Several persons writing within this perspective borrow freely and deliberately from the traditions of both feminism and liberation theology. Its most significant characteristic, however, is its predominant and deep concern with the ecological notion of "right relation," with the interconnections between queer theory and ecofeminism, and with the manner in which gay men must relate to nature and draw true sustenance from it. The gay body as site of meaning and spiritual revelation is also a key theme. Fundamentally, these are ethical questions, and the writers address them from the conventional vantage points of philosophy and theology, though with unusual twists.

The theology of these writers remains, at heart, an earth-based one, understood in its broadest sense of both the natural world and the human community. These two elements are considered inseparable from each other; there is an organic unity between them. One of its central motifs is that of liberation—not only for gay men, but also for all other persons and creatures who share this planet. There is an interesting gamut of approaches within the ecological mode of discourse. Its spectrum moves from the radical pantheism and separatism of Harry Hay and the Radical Faeries, through the American Indian androgyny of Will Roscoe and the sacred hedonism of Ron Long, to the ecofeminism of Daniel Spencer and the bleak existential theology of Michael Clark. While these may appear almost irreconcilable in outlook, it could be argued that there is a significant commonality between them. Each thinker is concerned first and foremost with the quality of the gay presence in the world, with the positive rapports that gay men can establish, as individuals and as a community, with the natural and social realms, and with the special gay "vocation" flowing from this. This is the meaning of "right relation." The androgynous theme—certainly present in Hay and Roscoe and, to a lesser extent, in Long and Spencer—is another aspect of the quest for "right relation," for the unity of difference and the special holiness of the gay body.

Ecological spiritual writing comes closest to a systematic theology of sorts. By raising the issues noted here, this form of writing seeks to address fundamental philosophical and ethical questions of meaning in a consistent, deliberate manner. Compared with the apologetic and therapeutic types, both of which are more reductive in their approach, the ecological mode is holistic in its perspective. It also brings together in a cohesive system a variety of discrete and apparently contradictory elements. Because of these elements, it can properly lay claim to a preeminent place among gay spiritualities.

One indication of the merging of ecology and spirituality in contemporary gay culture can be found on the Internet. A recent survey of gay spirituality Web sites revealed that almost one-third are concerned, either directly or indirectly, with issues about the earth and its welfare. This interest is significant, especially if one considers the almost nonexistent discourse about environmental issues found in mainstream religious institutions. It is also not accidental that a majority of these Web sites originate on the West Coast of the United States, where the influence of the New Age and of the environmental movement has been most keenly felt on American gay culture, and therefore on gay spirituality itself.

The fourth and final form of gay spiritual writing is *the autobiographical*. As the word indicates, the form has its roots in the lived religious experience of gay men, and in their reflections upon it. It is also a spirituality that mirrors, in fairly important and fundamental ways, the ongoing struggle with the ordeal of AIDS. It is personal in nature, very often focused on the person's religious upbringing, and concerned with the integration of this heritage in terms of one's psychological health and welfare. There is a certain "coming of age" quality about it. The argument can be made that this form of gay spiritual writing has blossomed at this particular time for two reasons. First, the existential fears emerging from the visceral struggle with AIDS raise intense questions of meaning. Second, greater mainstream acceptance of the gay experience invariably makes it possible for gay men to reposition themselves vis-à-vis their individual religious inheritance. Authors such as Malcolm Boyd and Andrew Sullivan, among others, write within the autobiographical tradition.[41]

Spiritual autobiography holds an esteemed place in most religious traditions. In the Catholic context, for example, one need only think of the writings of Augustine, Ignatius of Loyola, and Thérèse de Lisieux to understand the intimate connections between spiritual development and biographical self-disclosure. While one does not necessarily wish to suggest any close textual affinities between the writings of these Catholic saints and the somewhat less pious spiritual transcriptions of contemporary gay men, at the functional level they share a similar purpose. Essentially, both seek to explore and reveal the workings of faith—of the spirit—in human lives. In doing so, these writings serve a dual purpose: they deepen self-understanding, and they are exemplary models. In a sense, they provide the archetypal and personalized reference points without which any spirituality becomes intellectually and morally moribund. For the majority of gay men, these personal stories of religious struggle and insight undoubtedly hold the power to move and to inspire.

The autobiographical mode thus offers models for emulation, just as it purports to evaluate critically the continuing influence of institutional religion on gay lives.

If one were to step back and look at these four modes of discourse from a distance, one could perceive a certain continuum at play. I would suggest that it unfolds in the following sequence: from the autobiographical, to the therapeutic, to the ecological, to the apologetic. In other words, gay spirituality moves from the inside to the outside: from the most intensely personal and intimate (gay biographies and gay psyches) to the most explicitly public and historical (gay relations and gay generations). What is especially striking about contemporary gay spirituality is its all-encompassing nature: it tries to deal with oppression from every possible angle, covering every contingency, as it were. Gay spiritual writing does not shy away from the challenge posed by theodicy. If anything, it deals with it in a direct, almost aggressive manner. It takes as a given that the oppression of gays (and hence, the existence and adaptability of evil) was, is, and will continue to be a reality. In response, gay men have fashioned gods, as well as religious ways of being and modes of thought, characterized by their *totality*, almost as if they wanted no part of their lives to remain exposed or vulnerable. This is a predictable and laudable response to oppression. Not only is this good theology; it is a question of basic survival for gays as individuals and as fully contributing members of the larger human family. It also says a great deal about the creativity of the gay response to centuries of religious ostracism, and to the manner in which gay men have transformed the discourse of religious rejection into the language of spiritual empowerment.

## KEY CONCEPTS FROM DURKHEIM

Since the founding of sociology as a separate discipline in the modern pantheon of intellectual inquiry, religion has held an esteemed place.[42] The earliest sociological thinkers contended that religion, because of its overarching and influential position in society, was an especially rich and promising area of investigation for the sociologist. Almost from the beginning, therefore, there arose a field of study known as the sociology of religion. Those early thinkers were also perceptive. They sensed that religion, in its various historical manifestations, provided valuable clues to the nature of society itself. Since religion was a remarkably constant and recurrent trait of human social behavior, they were interested in understanding it for what it was: a human activity worthy of scientific analysis, in the same way that politics and the economy, for example, were studied and appreciated. For them, religion, given its cultural authority at different periods in history, could potentially hold the key to a fuller and more reasoned understanding of social forces.

Emile Durkheim, in his seminal work *The Elementary Forms of the Religious Life*, first attempted a systematic sociological reading of religion. His concern was with the "essence" of religion, and he argued that the nature of religious activity could best be understood by studying what he saw as the most "primitive" form of religion still in existence, that of the Australian aboriginal peoples, or what has been called totemism. As opposed to the intellectual approach of Max Weber,[43] the other giant in the field, Durkheimian sociology is a system emphasizing social solidarity and cohesion. The concept of society as a reality *sui generis*—something complete in and of itself—as the authoritative and independent embodiment of humankind's religious impulses, is the cornerstone of his social thought. His definition of religion is a remarkably social one: "Religious representations are collective representations which express collective realities; the rites are a manner of acting which take rise in the midst of the assembled groups and which are destined to excite, maintain or recreate certain mental states in these groups."[44]

The totemic principle in aboriginal religions refers to the religious embodiment of a clan's social identity. Basing himself on this observation, Durkheim argues that religion, as a universal mode of thought, is grounded in the human propensity and need for social order. Religion is therefore a cohesive force, and it reaffirms and sustains social cohesion by introducing a radical dichotomy between what is "sacred," or set apart, and what is "profane," or part of the everyday. The sacred, though highly "contagious," remains immutable and untouchable. The sacred, in a word, *is* society itself; more precisely, it is the power that society exerts over its members, and of which they are only dimly aware, if at all. Religion is society, and society is religion.

Durkheim describes certain social rituals that give rise to a collective awareness of the existence of the sacred. These rituals, meant to enhance tribal solidarities through an "acting out" of particular religious themes, produce states of ecstasy. He writes: "So it is in the midst of these *effervescent social environments* and out of this *effervescence* itself that the religious idea seems to be born."[45] These moments of social effervescence are geared to the production and maintenance of euphoric states of mind in the tribal individuals. The goal is the awakening of a feeling of an ultimate power external to the individual—for Durkheim, society itself—and its subsequent affirmation and vindication at the level of each person.

Two contemporary sociologists of religion provide further commentary on, and clarification of, Durkheim's understanding of "collective effervescence," particularly as it applies to ritual codes. Frederick Bird writes:

> Durkheim argued that collective effervescence often occurred when persons came together in a ritual setting and found in their group existence a contagious attraction and excitement absent when they were isolated from each other. Group rituals bring into life these otherwise dormant interpersonal forces, both because they allow persons to act in concert with each other and their group ideals and because they evoke and channel interpersonal affections.[46]

Hans Mol broadens the perspective, emphasizing the role of rites in binding individuals to a sense of sacred purpose or identity: "Rites articulate and reiterate a system of meaning, and prevent it being lost from sight. They act out and sacralize sameness. They restore, reinforce, or redirect identity. They maximize order by strengthening the place of the individual in the group, or society, and vice versa by strengthening the bonds of a society *vis-à-vis* the individual. They unify, integrate, and sacralize."[47]

This book takes a look at several aspects of contemporary gay life, and it proposes a reading of them that is informed and inspired primarily by concepts borrowed from a Durkheimian sociology of religion. Among these concepts, those of "effervescence" and "social rites" are particularly important. Classic sociological theory also suggests that religious behavior consists of three elements: belief, myth, and ritual. There are chapters dealing with each of these in turn. Paradoxically, the book also attempts to move beyond an exclusively sociological viewpoint. It suggests that gay spirituality is much more than a cultural or social manifestation: that it is, at heart, the enunciation of a vision of life, the calling forth of untapped resources and strengths innate to gay men.

# 3

# The Embodiment of Spirit

FOR A GAY MAN, acceptance by the dominant heterosexual world is never complete, nor is it ever an easy thing to learn to live without. One always feels a bit off balance, almost as though one were the last piece missing from the jigsaw puzzle. Heterosexuals may try to reassure us as much as they can, but they inevitably betray themselves, and they usually end up betraying us. All gay men have known at some point in their lives—and sad to say for some, for most of their lives—the feeling of being the outsider, the raw and stigmatizing experience of marginality. For some, it has scarred them forever; for others, it is a source of liberation and genuine relief.

Marginality and exile have emerged as two central images in gay spirituality today. In some important ways, these concepts hearken back to powerful themes in the Hebrew Scriptures about the rigors and challenges of being a chosen people, and how this privileged status is often paid for in blood and ostracism. Marginality is a most effective formative experience; it is the furnace that tempers the steel. Its corollary is loss. For most gay men, consciously or not, loss is the defining texture of our lives. Simply by having had to give up so much that so many others take for granted on an almost daily basis—whether family, children, lovers, acceptance, or inclusion—we have learned how to live on intimate terms with the experience of loss. In many cases, this experience has been sharpened to the point of exhaustion and rebellion by the overwhelming impact of AIDS on our lives and those of our loved ones.

Heterosexuals are lucky. They never really have to confront who they are in quite the same way that gays and lesbians do. The world is their oyster; it is made in their image. Their experience is, almost by definition, the experience of humankind. Gay men (and, yes, lesbians) do not have that luxury. Sooner or later, if they are to attain a state of balance and integrity in their lives, they will need to come out. They will need to declare who they are to themselves and to others. It is strange, when you think of it, how coming out places us in double jeopardy: we're damned if we do, and we're damned if we don't. Heterosexuals never have to declare themselves as straight. They simply are who they are: the overwhelmingly dominant standard of sexual behavior.

The older I get, the less tolerance I have for this dominant standard, and the more I need the company of others like me. I belong with these others; they are my family. We share the same history and the same roots. We have known the same fear and the same hatred. We have had to grow up with the same doubts. We have all had to hide ourselves and make believe. We have all known the anxiety of desiring a best friend, and we all have the emotional scars to show for it. In a word, we are the most precious and beautiful of survivors. I am proud of these brothers and of my need for them. I am proud of how far we have come together. I am proud of being one of history's outcasts, of having been burned with faggots in medieval Europe, of having stood in the cold morning rain at Dachau, of having been knifed by gang members in Los Angeles. I am proud, and I am angry—angry because there is no reason why any of this should have happened, and angry because such events continue to happen.

I cannot recall very many incidents of homophobia in my life, though I was taunted with the usual names as a child. Interestingly enough, I was an adult when these things began to happen—when I was confronted by people who were unhappy with things I might have done or decided, and who therefore turned to my being gay as a source of revenge. The most unsettling incident occurred the day I walked into a washroom at the university where I work and was confronted with large graffiti on the walls comparing me to a pederast and expressing thanks for my imminent departure. I was about to go on sabbatical. In itself, this example of cheap bathroom graffiti is not particularly uncommon. But I felt assaulted. I had a strong suspicion that a recent decision that I had taken in the context of my responsibilities at the university had been the occasion for this display of visceral dislike. My reaction was strangely instinctive. I quickly and almost comically began to erase the graffiti, as though it would remain engraved forever if I did not do so. I knew fear for one of the first times in my life. I was angry, and I resented the anonymity of the one who had done this act and gotten away with it. Such an experience is comparable, I would think, to that of women who are caught in a cycle of verbal taunting from men.

Calling someone a pederast, particularly a gay man, is the ultimate insult that straight society can conjure up. It is a scare tactic, meant to demonize difference and to imply that it acts in a predatory fashion in society. This is particularly striking when one remembers that, statistically, the vast majority of child abuse cases involve heterosexual men preying upon young girls. Children are perceived as society's most vulnerable members, the embodiment of the heterosexual's ability to create life and to propagate himself or herself. Imaginary threats against children—whether the accusations of the Roman Empire against the rites of early Christians, or those against the Jews accused of drinking the blood of Christian babies—have always been used as an emotional venue for expressing hatred and a means of building up genocidal mob anger.

Most gay men of my generation probably can recount similar stories. While the contours of these stories may be more or less dramatic, depending on the circumstances, they follow a similar narrative pattern of aggression (verbal or otherwise), anger, and defiant affirmation. Younger gay men or queers undoubtedly have a different experience and narrative. Their voice is perhaps less colored by this context of oppression and rejection, I would like to believe. In large part, this stems from their refusal to abide by the rules of normality, whether straight or gay. Situating themselves squarely and defiantly on the shifting margins of transgression, they can forever reinvent themselves and thereby subvert the dominant power discourse of homophobia. They represent, in what is certainly a rather ironic expression, "a moving target."

Such personal narratives inform and sustain gay spirituality. They are the strands and accents that make up its theology. In this context, theology should be understood as the systematic exposition of a collection of beliefs about what is perceived or defined as the sacred. Gay spirituality has a perspective on the sacred. Within this perspective, certain themes or images—certain understandings of what is holy and what is not—predominate. Gay spirituality also possesses a theology, a kind of edifice or hierarchy of the sacred, systematically exposing the premises of gay belief. Before it is anything else, however, gay spirituality is a clearly circumscribed historical phenomenon emerging from a specific culture. In its inspiration and influence, this culture is, without a doubt, unabashedly and unreservedly American, and from this important source, gay spirituality draws its theology and its rather unique view of the world—as does gay culture as a whole.

## AN AMERICAN DISCOURSE

Few gay authors have been as perceptive as Frank Browning in analyzing the religious dimensions of contemporary gay culture. In his two books, *The Culture of Desire* and *A Queer Geography*, Browning takes a close look at the values and paradoxes of this culture and proposes unusually insightful ways of making sense of it. Echoing the astute observations of Harold Bloom with respect to "the American genius for finding the divine within the realization of personal identity,"[1] Browning draws the following rather novel and intriguing parallel between gay liberation and U.S. Protestant evangelicalism:

> Evangelical Christians speak about "receiving Christ" and undergoing the rapture of the Holy Spirit, through which they, too, say they are born again. If the still new language of American gay liberation sounds remarkably like the Protestant language of reawakening and being born again, it is hardly accidental. For more than three hundred years American culture has been shaped by the paradigm of rebirth in the promised land. Queer activists' embrace of terms like "safe space" and "liberated zones" falls easily into that tradition, just as nineteenth-century utopian socialist communities did and as twentieth-century cultists do. As radically different as their particular faiths and ideologies may be, the underlying spirit is a profoundly American faith in rebirth, both individual and collective, in a place where we will come to a revolutionary comprehension of our place in relation to God or Nature.[2]

Although some born-again Christians might recoil at these similitudes being proposed, Browning is most perceptive in his analysis, for there can be little doubt that the religious paradigms that have shaped U.S. culture remain potent, including within the gay community itself. In a way, therefore, a very old-fashioned political motif is present in gay spirituality: it partakes of a long tradition of belief in the possibility of self-actualization and radical change, both individually and collectively. The personal and the political are different aspects of the one search for the sacred—a sacred ultimately found in the private space and identity of each autonomous citizen.

This self-actualization is the predominant theme in most gay spirituality, for one of its significant foci is the search for psychological health. In itself, coming out, the defining life experience for most gay men, is the epitome of self-actualization. Its similarities with certain aspects of the conversion experience are fairly self-evident. Gay spirituality—in fact, most gay discourse—attempts to legitimize the coming out process by reference to two powerful U.S. cultural norms: first, the individual has the obligation and the moral imperative to uncover his true self (the therapeutic); and second, the citizen has the obligation and the right to define publicly his identity (the political). To do both is to attain psychological health and balance. More important, it is to be a good person *and* a good patriot in the eyes of the divine godhead. It is a right stemming from divine election, and it is the sign of full political and religious citizenship, much as it was for the Pilgrim fathers.

Just as modern gay liberation has its origins in U.S. culture, so gay spirituality has its roots in, and draws its inspiration from, this same milieu. In this era, there can be little doubt as to the normative and universal qualities of the specifically Americanized gay culture. It is found, with slight variations, in most large urban areas in the West. Gay spirituality, however, is more than just another manifestation of this homogeneity. It is the expression of the particular element in the American character, as borne out by the history of the United States, that seeks definition of secular experience and identity in religious or quasi-religious terms.

The ability to invent oneself has always been understood as a defining element of the so-called American genius. It has given rise to a particular brand of identity politics that contrasts vividly with what is found elsewhere, most notably in Europe.[3] Gay spirituality probably could not have emerged from any other culture but American, with its mix of individualism and manifest destiny. The belief in the conflation of identity and the sacred, to paraphrase Bloom, provides naturally fertile ground for the emergence of a spirituality, or of forms of religious expression, tied not so much to faith and dogma, but to self-expression and self-realization. One example of such an attempt is the Harmonists of Christiansbrunn Brotherhood, a self-contained, marginal experiment in gay monasticism located in rural Pennsylvania. Its sole permanent members seem to be its two founders.[4]

The teachings of the Brotherhood are eclectic. Describing themselves as a "post-Christian religion," the Brothers limit their membership to gay men. Their general information brochure refers to them in the following terms: "We are a religious order of Single Brothers, androgynous as Adam in the beginning, now returning to take our place in the Garden, and understanding it for the first time. No longer children, now we are the Garden's guardian angels. We are the Woman of the Wilderness, waiting daily for the Divine Bridegroom to fill us and make us whole."[5] In one of their question-and-answer fact sheets, they further state: "As gay people, we have an intuitive sense as to what it means to fill and to be filled. We can use this by letting the Holy Spirit enter us in a literal sense. This holds true for men and women. It is a special relationship with the Holy Spirit, not creating physical life, but spiritual life."[6] These quotes offer a rather unique theological spin on the usual Judeo-Christian story of the Garden of Eden, and they propose an understanding of human nature and identity grounded in the somewhat abstract ideal of androgyny. The themes of penetration and procreation are here given a spiritual meaning.

The Brotherhood claims somewhat mystical origins in the person of Christian Renatus Graf von Zinzendorf, apparently the homosexual son of Moravian leader Count Nicholas Ludwig von Zinzendorf. Christian Renatus lived from 1727 to 1752. He was supposedly visited by Jesus Christ during his short life, and the two became lovers. A great deal of the theology of Christian Renatus was centered on the five wounds of Christ, and imagery of blood and penetration abounds. Filled with the Holy Spirit, in the literal as well as the spiritual sense, Christian Renatus acquired a monastic following called the Single Men's Choir, which became a source of scandal among Moravians. Christian Renatus was silenced, and his followers, it is claimed, fled Germany for Pennsylvania, where they established a cloister in the expectation that their teacher would join them, though he never did. After the death of Christian Renatus, the monastery fell apart. Today's Harmonist Brotherhood claims descendance from this lineage. Though the historical facts may be tenuous and more invented than real, such a "myth of origins" acts as a powerful legitimizing force in terms of the identity of any group, however marginal its status or outlandish its particular theological discourse. The myth also establishes lines of authority, and it provides a context for dogma and belief.

The Brotherhood appears to have few formal rituals, apart from spontaneous prayers, readings, and chantings at day's end in honor of Mother Earth. There is no monastic garb. The Brothers adopt an Amishlike approach to modern comforts, emphasizing self-reliance, farming, and crafts. They are not chaste. Sex is permitted only between Brothers, but one cannot take a lover. They follow the Six Fold Path, described as "the process by which the Holy Spirit comes to know itself and become enlightened."[7] Each day, the Brothers must focus on one of the six themes of perception, recognition, acceptance, judgment, change, and reflection. From this Path, it is claimed, comes the "discipline of behaviors, of how to act when one is One, the Holy Spirit."[8] These disciplines are threefold: empathetic (not blaming), patient (not shaming), and nurturing (not violent, either psychic or physical).

Similarities between the Harmonist Brotherhood and New Age–type religious movements are found at several levels. First, the reference to a golden time of innocence—in this case, the Garden of Eden—as both historical reference point and utopian vision for the group is a fairly standard motif in New Age thought. It is also not surprising that the members refer to themselves as guardian angels, since angels as intermediary beings between humans and the divine are common in New Age belief. Second, nature and the environment are omnipresent; Mother Earth and the Holy Spirit (this latter understood in terms of a manifestation or form of consciousness) appear to be the Brotherhood's primary divinities. They see themselves as having an important ecological mission of preserving, and caring for, nature. One detects here the strong influence of feminism and women's spirituality. Third, there is a prominent Eastern and psychotherapeutic flavor to the group's Six Fold Path. It is an eclectic mixture of Buddhism and popular psychology. This sort of eclecticism is one of the defining characteristics of New Age thought.

The Harmonist Brotherhood is another uniquely American experiment in the search for personal enlightenment and rebirth. As such, it shares common ground with all the other groups and individuals in the course of U.S. history—starting with the Pilgrim settlers—who have set out in the belief that they would create "a new heaven on earth," thereby ensuring their personal salvation.[9] Different or unusual in the case of the Brotherhood are its focus on gay men and the prominence of sexuality in its theology. Although some American communitarian movements in the past have adopted a rather liberal view of sexuality,[10] the Brotherhood is typically postmodern in its understanding of sexuality as a source of personal identity and as grounds for a legitimate spiritual quest. It is a very marginal manifestation of gay spirituality. As a social experiment, on the other hand, it is amazingly radical. It is almost totally an invention. Its understanding of history, its theology, its rituals, its discipline, and even its cosmology are fabricated either wholesale or from very disparate and sometimes opposing strands of thought. As Browning observes with reference to American religious movements in general, the Brotherhood proposes a revolutionary comprehension of the rapport of gay men to the sacred, and of the place they occupy in the world. It is a spirituality that is American to the core. In a strange way, the fact that it is also gay is almost secondary.

## A REDEMPTIVE DISCOURSE

The concern with salvation or redemption is a significant theme of gay spirituality. This is true not only of the more esoteric forms of this spirituality, but also of its mainstream variations derived from established (primarily Christian) theological thought. Such a discourse operates at several levels simultaneously: at its most basic and individualistic, in the imagery of coming out (i.e., self-acceptance) as a form of personal redemption; on the collective plane, in the notion of the gay community (the tribe) as a historically meaningful moment *and* movement; on the universal level, in the language of the unique "calling" or "vocation" of gays, which is not tied with the biological act of procreation; and even in the theological realm, with a sense of gays as the carriers of a special spiritual consciousness or revelation. One can add the ecological or the environmental: gays strengthen the social ecosystem ("save it") by virtue of the cultural diversity and creativity that they engender. It can be argued that contemporary gay spirituality, which is very much influenced, on the one hand, by the New Age concern with "consciousness" and, on the other, by ecological themes centered on environmental harmony, proposes the view that the kinds of sexual communities created by gays can be models for new types of ecohuman relations and social structures. This is founded on the argument (if not the prevalent belief) that gays play a unique role in the social ecosystem because they stand outside the norms of procreation and gender. Borrowing a dynamic and a law from the natural world, such difference is the source of diversity, which in turn strengthens the communal cultural gene pool.

An article entitled "Coming Out as Spiritual Revelation" expresses quite well this line of reasoning. In a somewhat grandiose tone, its author writes:

> We see a special role for gay people. In revealing that what looks weird, unnatural, queer or freakish is in fact another natural part of an unlimited and complex universe, don't gay people in coming out provide a key to a spiritual maturity for themselves and for others? What could be less useful in a soulless Darwinian world than individuals that don't procreate? Why in the world *are* we in the world? I believe we are here to reveal a further dimension of the diversity of life, and, in so doing, jolt our fellow human beings into celebrating life's differences.
>
> Moreover, I believe that gay people are here to witness to the truth that human life is not just about procreation, as magical and wonderful as it is. Reproduction is not the only mission for women and men. Just as God gave us a soulful dimension that binds us like a spiritual umbilical cord to the mother of creation and to each other, so she has created gay people to reveal this spiritual dimension.[11]

This passage is interesting for a number of reasons. First, it talks of "a special role," a unique vocation, for gay people. Implicit in such a statement is the sense that gays occupy a positive niche and perform a beneficial function in human history. This role, the author suggests, is tied both to the natural world and to the spiritual realm. One is a far cry here from the view of homosexuals as "unnatural" or "threatening" to the biological and social orders. It is important to underscore the word "vocation" in this context. This word is loaded with religious overtones. It refers to the notion of "having been chosen" as well as to that of "having made the choice to accept." This theme, it can be argued, is at the very heart of gay spirituality today, implicitly and explicitly. It reflects the wider essentialist-constructionist debate about the origins of homosexuality,[12] and it echoes the importance of the coming out process as both self-actualization and public statement.

A second element in this passage is the concept of biological and cultural diversity. The author argues that, even though gay people may appear to be "outside the norm," this very fact, by virtue of the diversity that it reflects and makes possible, is the source of considerable strength and value to the entire human family. This logic has its source in the biological sciences, and it is an especially powerful and persuasive one. It is widely accepted that biological diversity is essential to the maintenance of the ecosystem.[13] The less diversity the natural world enjoys, the greater its vulnerability. The author takes a scientific law and transposes it onto the cultural sphere, thereby augmenting, for many, the authority of his argument, while at the same time, and perhaps more important, locating homosexuality in the natural order of things. Gay theologian and psychotherapist John J. McNeill makes a similar biological argument: "The homosexual community has, perhaps, a special role to play in liberating the heterosexual community to a fuller understanding of themselves as persons by being *an organic challenge* within society to the partial and dehumanizing aspects of these [i.e., traditional] sexual-identity images."[14]

A third and final theme has to do with gay people existing in order "to reveal this spiritual dimension" of human existence. Essentially, this would occur via a kind of transcendence of the material world—in this case, as reflected in the natural act of procreation—by pointing to something greater and more valuable that lies beyond the world's utilitarian limitations. Even though gays may choose not to reproduce, and therefore do not reflect one of the so-called natural laws of existence, they perform a valid and much-needed role in human culture. This role, the author argues, is that of witness to the spirit. Gays carry a special spiritual consciousness, and they challenge other human beings to see beyond the closed boundaries of nature. This view of gay people as spiritual visionaries and cultural change-agents is part of a long tradition in gay spirituality. It was central to the theories of Edward Carpenter, and it continues to exert considerable influence even today. Harry Hay, for example, views gays as a third gender (in itself, an old Platonic idea) and argues that they are "assigned responsibilities for discovering, developing, and managing the frontiers between the seen and the unseen, between the known and the unknown."[15]

In a relatively recent book entitled *Gay and Gaia: Ethics, Ecology, and the Erotic*, American gay ethicist Daniel T. Spencer makes a compelling case for an ecocentric worldview and ethics rooted in the unique experience of gays and lesbians. His serious and important work brings together several years of reflection by a variety of theologians, both gay and nongay, and provides a comprehensive critique of traditional anthropocentric perspectives on nature. Spencer also seeks to define what is special or original about a gay and lesbian contribution to an ecological ethics. Stating that "the social location of lesbians and gay men at the fringes may be the best location from which to explore theologically the cosmos and our relation to the divine,"[16] he argues that such a contribution is fourfold: *embodiment* (which he defines as "paying attention to our health and integrity as body-selves and how this intersects with the health and integrity of our relations with others"),[17] *diversity* (in many ways, the distinguishing mark of the lesbian and gay experience), *disposability and dispensability* (the critique of which "stems from our long experience of being devalued and disvalued in mainstream society"),[18] and *appropriation without reciprocity* (stemming from "the social dynamics of the closet,"[19] which result in the gay and lesbian contributions to the common good being undervalued or ignored). Spencer is not really much different from other writers and thinkers who have attempted to redefine the gay experience of exclusion in terms of what it can contribute, in a positive and creative way, to universal human culture—in this case, to human ethics.

Gay spirituality relies heavily on the old Christian concept of grace. Sexuality is a gift from God, and it is a gift because of its varied manifestations. Being gay is therefore a blessing. This is a deliberate effort to counteract the traditional religious understanding of homosexuality as sinful, immoral, or worthy of damnation. What is important is that the individual accepts his true self, the self given by the godhead. In this is genuine psychological and spiritual maturity. Some even go so far as to claim that good theology is good psychology, and vice versa.[20] It is quite evident here that gay spirituality adopts the theme of "emotional-well-being-as-spiritual-illumination," which is prevalent in new religious movements of the psychotherapeutic variety.

Such a redemptive discourse has a strong Judeo-Christian flavor largely because it is Western in origin and inspiration, and therefore greatly influenced by such an ethos. A good example is the manner in which coming out, arguably the most significant moment in a gay man's life, is understood and analyzed as a religious experience. The individual acceptance and subsequent public declaration of one's sexual orientation are regarded as acts of faith in the godhead and as moments of intense spiritual revelation. The godhead would not have created same-sex attraction if it were not a good and necessary thing. In realizing and accepting this fact, the gay person, by overcoming self-doubt and self-hatred, is already saved. He has attained a holy state of self-awareness.

The other meaningful understanding of salvation in gay spirituality has to do with the gay community itself as a force for change in history. In this perspective, gay men are playing a critical role, particularly at this time of anxiety engendered by AIDS, in saving the world, as it were, from its intolerance and lack of compassion. It is argued that the gay community, in leading by example in the context of a serious medical crisis, becomes the agent of human salvation and a beacon of human virtue and merit. One reason gays can do this is their marginal status as sexual outcasts. In itself, this is a source of pride and an impetus for social and cultural change. In the well-chosen words of John J. McNeill: "At the heart of all gay spiritual life is a process of mourning and accepting our status as exiles in this world."[21] In addition, this work of salvation partakes of creation; it helps bring about the biblical "new earth."

This idealization of marginality is in itself redemptive. It is also utopian in that it argues for a view of history conditioned by the notion of perfectibility. A tenet of gay spirituality is the belief that gays, as a community, have a significant role to play in history as the prophetic voice of change with respect to gender and sexuality, and on the religious level as harbingers of a new spiritual consciousness. Moreover, by the very fact of their marginality and so-called unnaturalness, gays contribute to the diversification of the human species, thereby ensuring its strength and survival. These are interesting messianic motifs. But such a vision is essentially utopian. If utopia is, in its simplest sense, "the attainment of heaven on earth," then this vision, which is grounded in a perspective of absolute social equality, seeks to reclaim membership in the Garden of Creation for gays. This garden is not only a heavenly place; it is, first and foremost, the natural earth. Traditional millenarianism, on the other hand, looks to the consummation or redemption of history, often preceded by a great catastrophe or cataclysmic event. Some persons have suggested that the AIDS pandemic is this great event.[22] One must be extremely cautious about millenarian thinking. Gays must be on guard lest they speak, unbeknownst to them, the language of intolerance and divine retribution—the language of metaphor, the language of the enemy.

This imagery of redemption performs a meaningful role in providing legitimacy and credibility to the religious lives of gay men. Recasting the gay experience in the pseudotheological language of salvation accomplishes two important things. First, the discourse of gay spirituality is made to partake of an established and universal religious tradition, thereby ensuring a measure of veracity for its claims. Second, and perhaps more important, the social identity of the gay individual as a religious believer is considerably enhanced, thereby infusing it with a suprapersonal meaning. From a formal sociological perspective, therefore, gay spirituality can be said to operate both as a system of legitimation and, to a certain extent, as a system of socialization. In other words, it proposes valid norms of reference, and it ensures their positive internalization. It is functionally not very different from formal systems of religious thought and belief.

## An Incarnational Discourse

I am writing these words at a time of pain for gay men. One of our own was again martyred for no reason other than his sexual preference. A few weeks ago, in the backwoods of Wyoming, a young gay man named Matthew Shepard was murdered after having been tortured. The claim by his assailants was that he was coming on to them, hence their right to tie him to a fence and beat him senseless, leaving him naked overnight almost to freeze to death. Various explanations have been put forward about why this happened. They run the gamut from class differences to the inherent dangers of gay cruising.[23] This murder has given voice to opposing forces in U.S. society. On the one hand, there has been an increased call for hate crime legislation, while on the other, the rage of homophobia has continued unabated and has even reemerged in the disturbing picture of placard-carrying protesters disturbing Matthew Shepard's grave site. Not only does such a crime inspire revulsion and anger, as it should and as it must. It also gives rise to fear: fear of the most irrational, visceral type—a fear that makes you look around on dimly lit streets and avoid groups of kids walking toward you. It is not really a fear that paralyzes, but it is a fear that can nag you continuously if you allow it to go unchallenged. It reminds you of how brittle and superficial is the veneer of human civilization, and how easily supposedly rational individuals can turn into barbaric beasts. A Canadian lesbian journalist, writing in Toronto's newspaper *The Globe and Mail*, expressed it in the following way:

> Things die down; we await the next eruption. Such is the daily life
> of lesbians and gay men: completely accepted as a professor or a pig
> farmer or a waitress one day, facing incomprehensible violence the

next. If not to me, then to my friend. If not to my friend, then to the friend of my friend. So when a 21-year-old student such as Matthew Shepard is found tied to a fence post in Wyoming with his skull almost caved in, I fear for myself. That umbilical cord connects gays; it explains the emotional reaction to an event that happened south of the border, where the culture is different yet the same.... It's not the sort of fear that incapacitates you. It's a nagging, below-the-surface worry that dogs you when you're walking down the street, too afraid to hold a lover's hand.[24]

The hatred that Matthew Shepard inspired (let's not kid ourselves; that's exactly what it was) strikes us as irrational. "How can someone be murdered just because he was gay?" we ask with incredulity. Yet we are all to blame. Our homophobic culture is to blame. The ways we raise our children to be good little boys and girls—and nothing but—are to blame. The ways we mock and jeer the effeminate and the tomboy are to blame. The ways we subtly, and not so subtly, push the supposed values of home and hearth are to blame. The way we cringe when we see two men kissing on the movie screen is to blame. Our innermost thoughts of intolerance and dislike and sheer prejudice are to blame. We are all guilty.

Why do gay bodies elicit this kind of fear and panic? What do straight men especially find so repulsive in us, even when they are the objects of our attention, our flattery, and our desire? The most common explanation is that they see a reflection of themselves. They are afraid of being like us, as though it were something dirty and sick. So they strike out, trying to dislodge a reflected image of themselves, feeling powerless and vulnerable because of it. Another possible reason might be the manner in which gay men, simply by being sexually marginal, challenge and transgress societal norms of heterosexuality, thereby providing alternate ways of being in the world. This uncertainty and fluidity can leave many perplexed, sometimes finding its ultimately paranoid expression in queer bashing. Gay bodies push back the limits of normative discourses surrounding sexuality and identity. They challenge and threaten, just as they make possible new ways of thinking about the rapport between sex and spirit.

Queer bashing reminds gays, in the most violent way possible, of exactly who is in charge of the sexual norms. Queer bashing is the powerful reaffirmation of every straight person's—more precisely, every straight man's—obligation to define, establish, and police these norms, including the ultimate right to punish others for having dared to defy or overstep them. Queer bashing also keeps the anonymous others in line, sending a forceful message to all gay men and lesbian women that sexual norms are not to be trifled with, fundamentally challenged, or upset. In queer bashing, the body as limitless sexual possibility encounters the body as limited paranoid entity. The two find themselves caught in a sterile and ultimately deadly exchange.

The bashed body is the martyred body, at once victim and source of personal and collective redemption. This image of the gay body violently assaulted, broken and ultimately murdered, echoes the visual discourse of early Christian martyrdom. It finds its most perfect expression in the symbol of Saint Sebastian, an iconographic figure of immense erotic potential.[25] A more recent icon is that of Harvey Milk, the San Francisco gay activist and city supervisor who was gunned down in 1978, and whose witness still resonates very powerfully with U.S. gay men of a certain generation.[26] The murdered gay man assumes a visionary status and a redemptive power extending to all other gay men everywhere and for all times. This becomes especially evident when considering the manner in which those who have died from AIDS (not everyone, but only young, gay men) are portrayed. Their suffering and death—their martyrdom to political ineptitude and medical greed—assume a potency and a vibrancy that again devolve to other gay men by virtue of their membership in the same sexual community.

Body and spirit are one in gay spirituality. As was suggested earlier, gay spirituality is a "sexualized" spirituality. It advocates a positive outlook on the male body. In gay spirituality, the body—more specifically the experience of close sexual union—is the locus for encountering the sacred. This spirituality does not imply a dualistic or prudish view, as is too often the case with traditional Christian understandings of the body. Rather, it puts forth a holistic perspective, one conditioned by and expressive of the unique dynamics of same-sex erotic play. The gay body is seen as the embodiment of spirit. In a now classic essay, gay theologian Ronald E. Long expressed it in the following way: "Gay pride and gay courage—the courage to be gay—is rooted in the discovery of the holiness and sacrality of male beauty and gay sex. To be gay, in its deepest dimension, is in fact a religious vocation."[27] Gay spirituality is, in a word, an incarnational spirituality.

This encounter of flesh and spirit mimics Christian teaching, which posits the union of the godhead and the human person in the figure of the messianic God-man. Christian incarnational theology, significantly enough, is world-affirming. Because the divine "was made flesh," it raised this same flesh to the heights of divinity. Strangely, this is also disembodied flesh, in the sense that it is asexual. At the core of the Christian teaching, therefore, stands an unresolved neurotic paradox. The one significant difference between these two "theologies" is the total absence of a sexual dimension to the Christian God, whereas gay spirituality, in the words of Long, celebrates "the holiness and sacrality of male beauty." In making the male body a source of communion with the sacred, gay spirituality moves beyond Christianity—or perhaps it moves backward *from* Christianity—to a time undoubtedly more pristine and pagan in its inspiration, a time unencumbered by the anti-body prejudices of institutional Christendom. Gay spirituality poses a radical challenge. It proclaims the breaking through of the divine—its incarnation—in the very body that Christianity condemns: the "unnatural" gay body. It makes this "unnatural" body natural and good by investing it with religious meaning and purpose. The gay body is thereby transformed into the holy body, site of erotic and divine revelation.

Gay spirituality is characterized by three theological themes. As a form of cultural production, it is something uniquely American. It shares the values and aspirations of U.S. culture, more specifically its emphasis upon the expression of, and search for, the self as a legitimate religious quest. Second, as a spirituality that has its roots in the Western Christian tradition, its discourse is permeated with the imagery of redemption. Last, it is a pro-body spirituality. In particular, it views the male body and male sexuality as symbolic sites for an encounter with the sacred. These three elements provide a coherent basis from which one can begin to consider the multidimensional character of gay lives today.

# 4

# Myths and Symbols of
# Integration and Resistance

RELIGION IS AN ENDLESSLY amazing source of images and words that seize the imagination and fill it with fantastic stories and individuals. It has inspired and comforted, hunted down and terrorized, guided and sustained, even crushed and put to death. It has done all these things, yet it continues to fascinate and to shepherd in times both difficult and secure. The stories that religion recounts—its legends and myths—stretch back into the mists of time. They provide a universally accessible storehouse of human truths and offer paradigmatic models for human behavior. Religious signs and symbols give texture and meaning to these truths: a sort of visual shorthand that decodes their sustaining power. Not only religion possesses this rather extraordinary ability, though most assuredly religion continues to use it effectively. Other spheres of human activity—culture generally—are contexts for the production of myths and symbols; gay culture is one of them.

Perhaps gay men have a natural affinity for things religious. Perhaps the experience of marginality creates an acute sensitivity to the spiritual dimension of existence, as has been suggested by cultures and civilizations predating our own more skeptical one.[1] Regardless, I believe that the life stories of many gay men are replete with religious inspiration and religious struggle. These life stories are like templates that reveal the inner workings of the spirit. They can inspire us to a dialogue and to an engagement with our own religious impulses and upbringing.

I was a rather pious child and teenager, a fact that, even today, can cause a measure of consternation in people. Having been raised in a family context which, while not being overly Catholic, was nonetheless one in which the religious obligations of the church were important, I was fascinated, from an early age, with the outer trappings of religion. The habits of nuns and priests, the Latin of the mass, the holy images and lives of the saints, the rosary, votive lights, medals, and vestments—all these stirred my youthful and undoubtedly impressionable imagination. Mixed in with all this heady yet strangely comforting religious paraphernalia were boys. Though I was really not quite sure what the connection was, if any, between these two things, I sensed at an early age that there was something mysterious and not quite ordinary about both.

My first sexual experience was not until my early adulthood. I have vague recollections, however, about childhood episodes where parents of friends told me to stay away from their sons. I had obviously developed close friendships with these classmates, and something, whether my behavior or my attitude, triggered a defensive reaction in their parents. I do not think that anything overtly sexual happened, and if it did, I do not recall the episodes. But I do remember the strange feeling of rejection. It was a rejection made doubly painful by the fact that I could not fully comprehend what was happening. For me—as for any child—I knew only that I no longer had a "best" friend. This realization fed into my sense of solitude and difference, reaffirming my otherness.

Encounters like these account, in part, for the religious sensibility of gay men. They force us to turn, sometimes out of desperation and sometimes out of a genuine sense of spiritual need, to the security and meaningfulness of religious stories, symbols, and rituals. I do not want to propose that deprivation solely accounts for religious feeling, as some theorists have suggested.[2] Rather, I posit that a close affinity exists between the language and symbolic universe of religion and the performative discourse of homosexuality. Both, in a sense, provide opportunities and venues for us to undermine the normative and the ordinary. Both, in fact, summon us insistently to transcendence and to the creation of new languages and myths. Very often, this is a simple matter of necessity and of psychic survival. We need to develop—indeed, create—a symbolic world that resonates to the beat of our experience.

Like most Catholic young men of that era, I became an altar boy. This important step meant that I could participate in the symbolic world of

Catholicism in a much more intimate and direct way. I recall the struggle with memorizing the Latin responses, and the genuine feeling of accomplishment when I finally succeeded. There was a sense of mystery about the formulae, in part because I did not fully understand their meaning. The front-line, central role I played in the rituals of the church fascinated and engrossed me. It struck something very deep in me, and it resonated in a profoundly meaningful way. At home, I played at being a priest. I had arranged an altar in my room, forcing my brother and sisters to assist at my masses in the proper spirit of decorum and quiet. I attended, in turn, Catholic schools run by nuns and by the Salesian order of priests and brothers.[3] There I developed a strange crush on the boy-saint Dominic Savio.

Dominic Savio was a pupil of Don Bosco, founder of the Salesians. He died at fifteen, after a supposedly holy life of filial obedience and bodily purity. In the Catholic culture of pre-Vatican II, Dominic Savio and the girl-saint and virgin-martyr Maria Goretti were seen as exemplary for Catholic youth and were held up as models of chastity. I was smitten. Here was someone close to my age who had actually managed not to commit one impure sin in his short life, who had wanted to become a priest, and who had even been declared a saint by the church. He was my hero; I wanted to be like him. I also desperately desired to become a saint. My mother gave me a statue of Dominic, and I would light a candle in front of it on his feast day. I pushed my fascination one step farther. In a fit of religious zeal, I decided I would take a vow of chastity, just like my hero. Needless to say, my resolve did not last as long as I would have liked. Feeling quite guilty about my failure, I confessed my fault to a wise priest who was remarkably tolerant and patient with this idealistic folly of my youth. Looking back upon this episode in my early life, I can see the sort of erotic attraction motivating me. Dominic Savio was the perfect companion, a "special" friend with whom I could easily identify, and who could satisfy my religious fervor from the safe distance of his sanctity. He was also quite handsome. Images of him show an attractive youth with longish, slightly ruffled hair and sparkling eyes. Afraid and unsure as I was of the nascent sexual feelings in me, he and I could be chaste together. He was my first love.

At thirteen, I entered minor seminary.[4] My local parish was administered by a religious order known as the Blessed Sacrament Fathers, who were devoted to perpetual adoration of the eucharist.[5] Their kind of life appealed to me, and I decided to join the community. My years in seminary, and in the more intensely committed environment of the novitiate, were formative and decisive for me. Contrary to much that one hears about the sexual hothouses that are all-male boarding schools—much of it sensationalistic and somewhat vindictive—I did not have any sexual encounters, except for a single isolated one near my departure at the age of eighteen. The atmosphere of these places, however, was intensely charged erotically. As was the case with several of my classmates, I developed intense friendships that resonated with the camaraderie and unfulfilled desires of youthful urges. I recall one friend in particular. We were almost inseparable. In hindsight, I have a difficult time capturing the special quality that makes this one person stand out. I remember the time he told me that he masturbated. Somehow, this exchange created a singular bond between us, almost as though we had consummated the act then and there. This was an eye-opener for me—why, I do not exactly know. Perhaps it was the sheer effrontery of it, almost like confessing a secret sin in broad daylight; or perhaps it was the tingle and excitement from vicarious pleasure.

Seminary life is ritualized life. Every hour of every day is filled with activity, whether chapel, class, study, or recreation. I entered at a time of change for the Catholic Church, in the period of reform and uncertainty following the Second Vatican Council. My experience of seminary life was therefore radically different from that of my predecessors, who had to endure more structure and limitations, and who sometimes stumbled and fell under their combined weight. In my days, we were experimenting, and we often struggled with the very meaning of traditional religious teachings and ways of doing things. We became rebels at heart because we were encouraged to question and to express ourselves. If anything, we suffered from a lack of structure because the pendulum had swung a bit too far too quickly. At times, however, we were starkly reminded of just how little distance we had actually covered. One summer, while living in the community's house in New York City, I was taken to task by a superior for the length of my hair and for the inappropriateness of my having used my allowance to attend a performance of the controversial sixties' musical *Hair*. It was also a time of social unrest, and the heroes of my adolescence— Robert Kennedy, Martin Luther King, Dorothy Day, Daniel Berrigan— were voices that spoke eloquently to the necessary intermingling of religion and politics in the pursuit of the common good. I recall, after leaving the seminary, the euphoria I felt in burning my draft card.[6] I burned it, and then proceeded to bed the priest who encouraged me in this act of defiance. Something else was happening to me. I was discovering the equally necessary blending of the sexual and the political.

My tale is not mythical, though it serves the function of myth in my life. These years were and are paradigmatic for me. Quite apart from the romantic appeal and luster they still hold, they define and explain the gay man I have become. All gay lives are mythical and paradigmatic in the same sense. They all carry the unique experiences and qualities that not only make individuals who they are, but also define the life and times of a community. I may be different in the rather special way in which religion finds itself at the center of my life, though I suspect not. I suspect many of us carry a storeroom of religious symbols and images that continue to speak in very powerful and prolific ways to the texture and sense of our lives today. As a community, gay men, I believe, need to create myths and symbols for themselves. They may do this through a living spirituality, or they sometimes may choose to adopt a far more secular approach.

This chapter examines some of the myths and symbols of contemporary gay life, and attempts to understand them from a religious or, at the very least, a pseudoreligious perspective. The first section considers myths of origin, ways in which we choose to define and make sense of our place in the world, more specifically from the vantage point of history. The next section discusses myths of community, or how our vision of ourselves as members of a group has impacted on gay lives and the notion of a gay identity today. My choice of the word "myth" does not imply something untrue or false; rather, I use it in the restricted and more accurate sense of a "paradigmatic model," a view common in the scientific study of religious phenomena.[7] The final section deals with symbols, those of integration and those of resistance. This duality reflects the contemporary gay experience.

## MYTHS OF ORIGINS

Individuals as well as communities need a sense of where they come from and of their place in the world. At the individual level, we talk of our past, our families, and the influences, positive or negative, that have shaped us. This is relatively easy to do, in part because our lives are more neatly circumscribed. We are looking at one individual whose life experience remains considerably limited by circumstance and by longevity. For a community, however, the picture is understandably more complex and requires a greater degree of analytical sophistication. Communities are living entities comprising a wide and disparate collection of individuals, all of whom have their own stories and perceptions of where they fit into the broader social dynamic. There is seldom a shared and indisputable sense of how and why the community came to be, and even less of where it may be headed.

The gay community qua community is a relatively recent phenomenon, as is the understanding of the homosexual person qua homosexual. Yet gay men have always been intensely preoccupied with origins. This preoccupation assumes many forms, several of which are concerned with providing legitimacy to the gay experience by uncovering or suggesting examples from the past that can serve a mythical role in the formulation of a gay sensibility. The function of myth is to supply models for human behavior. Myths define and set the fundamental paradigms for all subsequent human activity; they establish the order of things in the here and now by explaining how things were created "in the beginning." These paradigms function as blueprints. Not only do they propose ways of behaving, however; they also structure and delimit reality by suggesting and imposing explanations for why things are the way they are. In sum, myths create meaning. They are as real and as effective as any other form of human cultural production.

I recall with acute intensity the time in my early adulthood when I discovered that there had existed great gay men in history. Whether it was Socrates, Alexander the Great, Michelangelo, Leonardo da Vinci, or Shakespeare—the names rang with pride in my imagination. They said something very positive, not only about the kinds of contributions others like me had made to human civilization, but also about myself as a gay man. They reminded me that everything was possible, and that I could accomplish something equally significant and meaningful despite—or perhaps even because of—my particular proclivity. When I also encountered the possibility of nurturing and positive male relationships such as the biblical one of David and Jonathan, for example, or the intense camaraderie of the legendary Spartan soldiers, I began to glimpse the attainability and beauty of love between men.

Whether or not these historical figures really were homosexual—or even whether or not they existed—is almost beside the point. What is important is that they serve as exemplary models. They function as a source of inspiration and as images that sustain the emergence of a gay identity. In this sense, they are "mythical." They offer examples that can be imitated and even copied. They also act in an apologetic manner. By reclaiming and reappropriating these men as important historical figures whose sexuality was germane yet incidental to their accomplishments, gay historians have provided the prolific symbols and models necessary for the demarcation of a modern gay identity. In mythology, the hero was a sort of demigod, standing between the restrictively human and the more exalted and limitless divine. Gay heroes are the same. They reaffirm the possibility of human accomplishment as a function of sexual difference, and they enunciate the real likelihood of transcendence through this simple fact. Gay heroes are like demigods challenging each of us, in turn, to undertake a journey similar to theirs. They are mythical beings, original in the dual sense of "at the beginning" and "creative."

Apart from heroic historical figures, gay mythology includes personages of fantasy and desire. Which gay man does not remember those images of his youth that provided fodder for his nascent sexual yearnings? Very often, the boyish reaction to those images was irrational and unconscious. We simply liked looking at half-naked gladiators or hunky cowboys, or hanging out with the class bully, without knowing what it was about them that excited or disturbed us. Was it a sense of adolescent adventure, as we so often thought? Unlikely. The images were, at one and the same time, iconographic and sexually stimulating. They provided objective, aloof models of masculinity and manhood to which we responded with the uncertainty and rawness of our still incomplete erotic selves. An icon is a symbol associated with sacredness. Not just the image, but the very object itself, carries divine power. In the pangs of youthful desire and admiration, we encountered a sense of the sacred, of an erotic power and fire with the unique potential to make us whole human beings. We discovered male beauty and sensuality and, in so doing, caught a glimpse of what was holy in our lives.

Gay pornography, despite the accusations of selfishness and degradation leveled against it, partakes of a similar process of "sacralization." Its images are the expression of "the sacrality of male beauty and homosex," to borrow the very apt expression of Ronald E. Long, who also describes this unique attraction in liturgical terms:

> [There is] a susceptibility—indeed, an erotic receptivity—to masculine beauty at the heart of many a gay man. And it is this receptivity I argue that grounds a gay identity for most gay men. The theme

of male beauty is a vastly underplayed theme in current theory. I would here place it in the forefront of analysis. Being gay is not simply a matter of erotic interest in other males, but of a responsiveness to the beauty of other males, a responsiveness that includes the sexual. For gay men, I submit, there is a compulsion in a magnificent male that commands attention and solicits . . . the word "worship" will suffice for the moment. And sexual interest here may be seen as a mode of such worship.[8]

Gay pornography frames the discourse of male beauty, thereby defining the parameters of what (or who) must be worshiped and how. The appropriate liturgical responses are those of adoration and thanksgiving. Every time that gay men consume pornography, they engage in a liturgical celebration of the body beautiful, of the male body as site of transcendence and sacredness. This does not apply exclusively to the porn star, however. Beautiful men are everywhere, and our response to them can be equally sacramental. We worship the beauty of maleness itself, as it is incarnated in every man.

In addition to the mythical constructs offered by gay heroes and gay pornography, certain key events define the gay community as a whole and provide it with the reference points necessary to its historical legitimation and to its standing as a postmodern cultural movement. Three of these are the trials of Oscar Wilde at the end of the nineteenth century, the imprisonment and extermination of homosexuals in Nazi concentration camps during World War II, and Stonewall. Each can be said to have been at the source of the contemporary gay condition in the West and its concomitant quest for identity. Each has been the origin of images and symbols that are mythical in the sense of paradigmatic and have made possible a strong gay culture in this century.

Oscar Wilde is making a comeback these days.[9] In movies, books, and plays, the greatest English-speaking aesthete and literary figure of his era is emerging as the martyr of Victorian bourgeois intolerance and prejudice. Several scholars claim that the modern homosexual was not understood as a distinct social category until Wilde's trials.[10] The trials literally created a person who could be labeled "homosexual" by fixing identity at the intersection of sexuality and gender. They made possible a separate homosexual identity as a recognized (if not necessarily legitimate) way of being in the world. For the first time in history, individuals erotically and emotionally attracted to others of their own sex could make this attraction their primary focus in defining who they were as persons. Not only did this blow away several negative myths about homosexuality; it also created a whole series of positive ones that still resonate with many gay men today. Foremost among these are the strongly held beliefs that we are defined by the objects of our affection, and that we can lay claim to a social difference based on this fact. In the public trials and persona of Oscar Wilde, traditional (and hypocritical) bourgeois sexual respectability encountered most dramatically the subversive discourse of "the love that dares not speak its name." From this clash there emerged the modern homosexual, a character whose sexuality *was* his identity, and whose birth pangs were the harbinger of much more profound social and cultural change.

Difference also accounted for what is arguably one of the most devastating yet strangely misunderstood tragedies for gay men in the twentieth century: their imprisonment and extermination in Nazi camps during the 1930s and 1940s.[11] In his powerful play *Bent*, which takes place during this era, Martin Sherman uses Dachau as the site for an encounter between two different kinds of homosexual men. Max, a somewhat jaded individual who prefers to wear the yellow Star of David rather than the pink triangle meant to identify homosexuals (because he claims that he is not really a "fluff," in the quaint language of the times, and also because he believes that Jews are less stigmatized in the camp hierarchy of prisoners), is forced to watch while another prisoner, Horst, who is also his lover and who has taught him that it is important not to feel in order to survive, is killed for the sheer sport of two guards. Max is then left to dispose of the body of his lover. As he drags him away, the camp siren sounds. In an image reminiscent of the *Pietà*, Max must stand at attention for two minutes with the dead body of Horst in his arms. It is the first time that the two men can freely touch, and Max finally declares his love over his lover's corpse. As Max moves away from the shallow grave in which he has deposited the body of Horst, he stops, walks back, and jumps into the hole. He emerges with the coat of his dead lover bearing the pink triangle and exchanges it for his own. He then deliberately electrocutes himself while reaching for Horst's cap, which Horst had earlier been forced to throw onto the barbed wire fence, and which had led to his death.

This scene is profoundly touching and disturbing. Many levels of religious symbolism are at work here. It is a scene that speaks of self-acceptance, redemption, and the grace and wonder of human love (and, yes, divine grace) in the most dehumanizing situation. It is primarily and most eloquently, however, a scene of defiance. Defiance is good and necessary and very much human. It becomes especially so when one has been the innocent subject of willful condemnation and vilification, of imprisonment and torture, of exile, burnings and, as expressed forcefully in *Bent*, systematic extermination. This disquieting period of history for gay men has reminded us that we can still be hated and killed for our love. It serves a mythical function of remembrance, which is a critical factor in the formation of a community—so critical that a community without a shared history is a community without a future. It has done this most forcefully through the proud and defiant appropriation of one important symbol of this hatred, that of the pink triangle.

Several years ago, on a stopover in Munich, I visited Dachau with my lover. We walked silently around the remnants of the work camp, preserved as an eloquent monument to the human spirit and a stark reminder of human evil. I recall most vividly the exhibition in the entrance hall. German schoolchildren on a field trip were talking loudly and walking about with Walkman earphones on their heads. Somehow, I felt that their oblivious behavior was violating the sacredness of the place. In the display, someone had included a pajamalike uniform of one of the camp inmates. To my sadness, joy, and pride, I saw that there was a pink triangle sewn on it. Tears welled up in my eyes. I felt at one with the anonymous gay man who had been forced to wear this uniform in this horrid place in the none too distant past. I felt at one, and my defiance made me love him. If not for the fortunes of fate, I told myself, that could have been me or someone I loved. In the gay consciousness, what happened at Dachau or in places like it does not loom large. It is as though we wanted to forget, certainly a necessary, though dangerous, response. We are better at marking the joyful moments of our history, and appropriately so. We would also do well, however, to recall the tragic and desperate times when we were pariahs.

For many gay men, particularly those who share an Anglo-American cultural frame of reference, the Stonewall riots of June 1969 mark their political emancipation. This event looms very large in the consciousness of gay men, though it must be remembered that it serves an exemplary and paradigmatic role rather than a historically causal one. Stonewall heralded the end of an era and the beginning of another. It was the first time that gays—and more specifically the most marginalized of gays: transvestites, transsexuals, and hustlers—responded directly and decisively to the continued harassment of the police, who were, and still are, the most visible agents of the normative social order. As such, it had a purgative and a catalytic effect. At the level of myth and symbol, it denotes defiance and anger. Functionally, it occupies a role similar to that of other "revolutionary" moments in history associated with such events as the birth of nations and of ethnic or cultural communities.

Even today, the gay pride marches that celebrate the anniversary of Stonewall are occasions for a symbolic reenactment and reinforcement of its mythical stature as a defining historical moment for the gay and lesbian communities. The blatant public display of same-sex affection, cross-dressing, and gender-bending retells and reframes the defiance of the Stonewall pioneers, though now obviously in the form of a discourse considerably less radical and better suited to a uniformly commercialized culture. These marches and public demonstrations are meant to re-member, that is, to bring together, once again, the disparate elements of our community, and to restage the unity that Stonewall imparted to us all.

We need myths of origins because stories impart meaning and power. In their telling and retelling, we come to an understanding of ourselves as a people with a common history, and less as lone individuals with disparate and unconnected life cycles. History imparts pride, and pride makes change possible. Whenever we celebrate or honor an individual or a formative event from our past, or write or sing or dance about it, we strengthen the future of our community. Some years ago, I visited Oscar Wilde's grave in Paris, where I deposited a single red rose. In doing so, not only was I paying my respects, but I was also making a public statement about who I was and how much I owed my sense of self as a gay man to Wilde. In a significant way, he was my ancestor and spiritual parent. I, as his son from the late twentieth century, knew I needed to reclaim his shameful though proud legacy as my own.

In these myths of origins—heroes and icons, moments of tragedy and those of celebration—gay men discover their history and place in the world, and through them they are able to enter in communion not only with their ancestors, but also with the spirit that animates their lives, both individually and collectively. This need for "a human space," defined by the variable of historical time, is a spiritual craving born of human contingency. By acquiring a sharper and more refined sense "of whence they come," gay men are better equipped to know "that to which they aspire."

## Myths of Community

To claim that one is gay implies that one is also part of a community of men who are alike. Though one can speak of being a homosexual as something personal and private—that is, as something that can be limited, in theory, to the isolated sex act—being gay necessarily connotes the existence of a group or community beyond the discrete self. This community colors, to a significant extent, the understanding of the "gay" self. In other words, "gay" is a social construct. It cannot be properly grasped—or lived out, for that matter—without reference to the context within which it is operative, the gay community itself.

There is remarkable strength in community, just as there is uncommon pride. When, as an adult, I first came to the difficult realization of what I was, I remember the unexpected relief and happiness I found in being with others like me. Equally important, I had a great sense of adventure in discovering that, as a gay man, I had a history that went far beyond my little part of the world at this particular point in time. I avidly gobbled up all I could read about gay history, as I continue to do to this day. When I went out, alone or with friends, the energy and validation I experienced in being with other gay men only reaffirmed my sense of belonging, as it does now. As "out" gay men today, we experience this on a regular basis in our daily lives. Such a feeling of complicity accounts, in large part, for the pleasure we find in the company of other men. The act of looking into the eyes of another gay man walking toward you on the street implies an unspoken recognition and an interconnection that are profoundly affirming yet strangely enticing. Cruising is the affirmation of our difference and also of our potentiality. It places us in instant communication with "the other who is like us," this other who is a latent source of intimacy and transcendence, and who can be the occasion for our giving of self.

We are a sexual community. Our bonds are primarily a function of our physical attraction to and for one another. We are also a sexualized community. We have chosen to define ourselves as a grouping of individuals whose primary affinities are based on the fact that we are erotically and affectively drawn to other men, and the larger culture often chooses to see us in this way. The parameters we set for ourselves are translated into the boundaries fixed for us by society, while these same boundaries condition our sense of who we are. Today, we have become an extremely lucrative market niche, with advertisers bending over backward to appeal to our

disposable incomes and to our apparently highly developed sense of con-
spicuous consumption. Whether it is boys in underwear or naked torsos
pushing a particular fragrance, advertisers capitalize on sex and our attraction to men in a blatant attempt to entice us to buy and buy ever more. Our
community is as much a commercial community as it is a cultural or a
political one.

In this environment our myths of community—the images and archetypes that sustain our communal roots—become ever more precious and
necessary. At one level, they act as safeguards, protecting our integrity and
identity as a group. They tell us who we are in a fundamental sense, and
they reaffirm our value and worth in the wider world, which is often not
supportive and appreciative of our difference. On another level, these
myths challenge us. They call us to be more and better than we are. They
remind us that through the experience and the craving for community, we
attain transcendence, and we are finally able to grasp the inescapable,
almost instinctive, need we have for one another as men who love other
men. We find solace and healing in this fact. It is who and what we are at
heart.

It may be read as an offensive and irresponsible statement to some in
these days of sexual panic, but I profoundly believe that we need to
reaffirm our heritage of promiscuity. We need to reclaim our status as sexual deviants. I say this not because I want to shock others or I expect that
we will all run into the streets and fall upon the closest available man, but
because we must remember that we are part of a historical community that
has consistently challenged and subverted the sexually normative. Though
this has been the source of our oppression and our rejection, it has also
forged us as "a nation unto ourselves," a mirror held up as a challenge to
the (hetero)sexually commonplace. We have turned masculinity upside
down, challenging its monopoly and its arrogance, and further declaring it
to be defiantly and unmistakably our own. We have pushed it to such an
extreme that we have made a parody of it, wallowing in its excesses while
poking fun at its serious contradictions. We have existed in order to
remind the straight man and the patriarchal social order he has created
that he is not the apex of creation or the *summum bonum*. We still do. He
has hated and killed us for it. He still does.

Our most fundamental archetype is that of transgression. Strangely
enough, it also reveals itself as the primary source of our power and our
enduring difference. These days, however, we seem to want to be the same

as the straights. We talk of being part of their military machine, of copying their marriages, and of raising progeny like them. There can be no doubt that, as with all other human beings, we should have these rights if we so choose. The more serious question is whether, in so doing—and in doing it *on their terms*—we are not being pulled away, quite intentionally, from what is properly our role as sexual gadflies. Our power and our difference are functions of our status as outsiders and as "perverts." To give this up makes it almost impossible for the sexually normative to be challenged. Who else can do it? And who else can do it so radically, so disturbingly, and with such a campy sense of class as we can? Michel Foucault has exposed persuasively the mechanisms by which the social order controls and manipulates sexual power and sexual agency.[12] We do well to remind ourselves of his prophetic words, as queer activists maintain.

In a passage from his beautiful book *Love Undetectable: Notes on Friendship, Sex, and Survival,* Andrew Sullivan offers an incisive commentary on one of the most hotly debated features of the contemporary gay urban scene, that of the circuit party. He reflects on his first such party and on the broader topic of masculinity:

> While the slim and effeminate hovered at the margins, the center of the dance floor and the stage areas were dedicated to the most male archetypes, their muscles and arrogance like a magnet of self-contempt for the rest. But at the same time, it was hard also not to be struck, as I was the first time I saw it, by a genuine, brazen act of cultural defiance, a spectacle designed not only to exclude but to reclaim a gender, the ultimate response to a heterosexual order that denies gay men the masculinity that is also their own.[13]

Sullivan reminds us that, even in the midst of one of the most outlandish and contested of our public rites and celebrations, our irrepressible spirit of defiance manifests itself. Despite its having become increasingly mainstream, gay culture manages to retain its subversive edge. It succeeds in reclaiming as its own, and even in surpassing, the impossibly high physical standards by which we have traditionally been ostracized. The gay bodies dancing with abandonment at this party have become the almost perfect expression, and therefore the fulfillment, of these same standards. They have subverted masculinity by exceeding it. One of the stranger ironies about contemporary society is that "the gay style," whether in fashion or in forms of entertainment, has become the preferred cultural medium for heterosexuals. Although this may not necessarily indicate a more enlightened acceptance of homosexuality—and it certainly does not—it points to the extraordinarily persistent influence of so-called gay aestheticism, and to the social stature that gays have managed to attain because of our buying power. It can be a double-edged sword, however. In having and flaunting so much disposable income, do we thereby feed into the straight paranoia about our growing influence? Do we really need to care about this? I think not.

Over a period of eight months, I volunteered once a week at a local AIDS hospice. It would be a cliché and somewhat untrue to claim that it was a difficult experience, though it was at the beginning. I had wanted to do something like this for a long time. Ever since the onslaught of the epidemic, I had felt that I needed to do more than give money and wear a red ribbon as an all-too-facile expression of solidarity. I considered myself unduly and inappropriately distant from the front line in this war, not without a tinge of good old-fashioned guilt and remorse. Time away from my professional work afforded me the chance finally to commit myself and to resolve some of this anxiety.

My first few weeks brought a wave of emotions stemming from my encounter with death and the degeneration of the human body. Like most first-time volunteers, I became excessively obsessed with cleanliness. Though I knew all about universal precautions and the basic biological facts of transmission, I became anxious when I came in close proximity to bodily fluids and had to handle them. My reaction, I knew, stemmed from an irrational, though understandable, fear of contamination. Forcing myself to overcome my phobias, I discovered that I could also experience moments of great tenderness. I will never forget the first time that I held a dying man in my arms as his diaper was being changed. He had only a short time to live, and his skeletal body felt as light as a sheaf of paper. He was beautiful. Somehow, then and there, I knew that the disease was not about hopelessness and desolation; rather, it was a summons to all of us to selflessness and care for one another. It was a clarion call to the conscience. It was a test of our humanity, a moment of grace that we could either rise to or choose to ignore. We mercifully chose the former.

All of us have experienced to some degree the painful loss and desolation that these times have forced upon us. Yet we have emerged as a resilient and caring community. The energy we expended and the institutions we established in order to take care of our own have been exemplary. We have rediscovered what has always been one of the hallmarks of our community, but we somehow lost sight of it in the heady days of disco and the clone look: we are, in fact, a generous, hospitable people.

John J. McNeill speaks of "the spirit of hospitality" as a gay virtue, referring to "the extraordinary outpouring of love on the part of the gay community to all the victims of AIDS, an outpouring which is one of the greatest manifestations of hospitable love in our day."[14] It is no accident that we have taken so easily to this obligation of care forced upon us by circumstances. We have often cared for one another in silence and exile, away from the prying and judgmental eyes of a sexually anxious world.

Today, one often hears severe and recurring criticism of the gay community, not only from gays themselves, but from society at large: that it is too blatant, too exclusive, too commercial, too jaded, or too radical, to list only a few such observations. At times, some of these perceptions are certainly true, though I doubt they are so generally. My personal favorite—though its implications can be frightening—is that we are too powerful. Interestingly, it is only when formerly powerless groups begin to acquire a modicum of acceptance and influence that we hear this sort of language, much like the sexist line about feminism having destroyed the family or castrated the modern male. It is the rhetoric of fear and insecurity, and one that we should never reconcile ourselves to lest we be forced to crawl back into the dark ages of self-doubt and invisibility as a community.

Our community is many things at once: sexual, transgressive, masculine, and caring. As sexual beings, we celebrate and flaunt our masculinity, the better to subvert its impossible claim on all of us. We are marginal beings, and this marginality makes it feasible and necessary for us to challenge the heterosexual norms that fix and dictate so much about the world around us. We are a community of solidarity, reaching out to those among us who suffer and are rejected. We are also an angry community, for we know firsthand the hatred and disdain that cause the unnecessary suffering of our dying brothers. We need to reaffirm and reclaim these qualities of community—these archetypes—that too often we tend to view either as negative traits or as unreasonable goals to be achieved. This can and should include our righteous anger. These "myths" can activate and sustain our imaginations, both as proud gay men and as persons sharing this earth with other human beings. Speaking of gay myths of community in no way intimates that we stand removed from the legitimate concerns of others; rather, we stand prepared to help them fashion a better world for all.

## Symbols of Integration and Resistance

As gay men, we occupy a dual and, at times, uncomfortable position in society. We very much want to be accepted despite our difference, and we want to live, and love, and even propagate, at times, like the rest. In many respects, depending on the given environment, we can do these things quite well and quite confidently. We can live quiet lives, perhaps not of desperation, but ones marked by a modicum of normalcy. In other words, we want to be part of it all, to be integrated, and to share the social world of human beings. This is certainly understandable. There can be little doubt that we should be allowed to participate fully, like all citizens, in the lives of our neighborhoods and to contribute to the vitality and welfare of our communities. There is, however, an opposite pull in us, one that I believe is equally strong and compelling in its allure, even though we do not like it and we very often resist it. This "pull" places us in a position of exile, existentially and spiritually.

We know we are fundamentally different, and we know in our innermost souls that we will never be fully accepted, despite the positive-sounding rhetoric of our supporters and the tangible benefits we may achieve through our politics. This difference need not imply that we will never attain equality. On the contrary, it should be viewed as the expression of an existential reality, and it can and should be accepted as a source of pride and vigor. Gay spirituality does not argue that we are here to become "like the other"; rather, it asserts that our very "otherness" and difference are the special gifts we bring to this same other. We are called to cherish and celebrate our originality. In doing so, we invariably place ourselves, at times, in a position of violation and resistance, and we would do well to remember that the nonnormative is very often the best able to effect genuine social change, just as the guerrilla fighter in the hillside challenges his society by standing outside it.

Integration and resistance are parts of the common experience of most gay men of my generation. We have struggled with its contradictions in very real ways. Some have lived to tell the tale; others have left us in their wake, silently nurturing our terrible grief at their unexpected departure. Born in the blandness and conformity of the 1950s, we came of age in the freedom and rebellion of the 1960s, experienced the exciting sexual license and excesses of the 1970s, only to be slapped hard and struck down by the great plague of the 1980s and 1990s. In this brief span of some fifty years, we have gone from one sexual and political extreme to another, pulled in radically opposite and seemingly irreconcilable directions. We marched at Berkeley and Stonewall, haunted the baths and sex bars of San Francisco and New York, and cared for our dying lovers and friends in the urban enclaves of Los Angeles, Toronto, and Montreal. We have been, and still are, a war generation, that of Vietnam and that of AIDS. We have not been, and are not, like the countless others. We do not want to explain. We do not want to have to justify ourselves, to smile the smile of the smug and the excruciatingly normal. For, in not doing so, like warriors and soldiers of every era, we pay homage to our dead comrades. Reflecting on the parallels between the intense camaraderie of war and that caused by the devastation of AIDS, Andrew Sullivan writes:

> The awareness of the deaths of one's peers, and the sadness they evoke, and the pain you are forced to witness—not just the physical pain but all the psychological fear and shame that AIDS unleashed—all this was slowly building a kind of solidarity that gradually ruled my straight friends out of the most meaningful part of my life. There comes a point at which the experience goes so deep that it becomes almost futile to communicate it. And as you tell them less and less and experience more and more, you find yourself gravitating to the people who have experienced it as well, the ones who know instinctively, the people to whom you do not have to explain.[15]

I found out only a short time ago that my first lover died of AIDS. We had lost touch over the years, and the only hint I had that something was wrong with him was an obscure chain Christmas card I received one year alluding to his struggles with his health in the course of the year just passed. I read between the lines. We had a wonderful, though brief and strained relationship, and I was very much in love. It is fair to say that he changed my life. He was the reason I came out, the first to show me that it was possible to fall madly in love with a man. I left a comfortable, close relationship with a woman for him, and we moved forward on our own, somewhat blindly and romantically. The pain when it all fell apart—as it had to—was excruciating. I eventually had to move to another city, in large part because I very much needed to get away from him. He lingered on the edges of my life, resurfacing every now and then in a telephone call on New Year's Eve or an obscure letter or postcard.

The news of his death was given to me *en passant* at a dinner party. I literally felt as though I had been punched in the face. I did the only thing I knew to do that night. I got drunk. There were obviously a number of questions tearing at me, not the least of which involved my own vulnerability and mortality. I am not the first gay man, nor am I the last, who will experience this sort of thing, though I hope it will become less frequent over time. Nor am I the first or the only gay man to have lost a lover or a friend to AIDS. There is nothing unique or particularly ennobling about all this. I stand as part of a living chain of others like me—brothers in death, all—who have seen the important people in their lives brought down and ravaged by this virus. Ultimately, this death bound me irrevocably and defiantly to these others. Though I had known people around me who had fallen to AIDS, this was the first time that someone with whom I had shared an intimate relationship had died because of it.

What are the symbols of gay lives today? AIDS is undoubtedly one of the most compelling and most dramatic, and it could even be said to be the premier one. In saying this, I am conscious of the need to explain carefully what I mean. I am making a loaded statement, one that could lend itself easily to misinterpretation. In stating that AIDS is our fundamental symbol, I *do not* wish to imply that we should accept it as the sum total of our lives, as the one and only thing that defines and sustains our identity and our purpose. That, I believe, would be wrong and indecent. Nor do I mean, as is the case with so many righteous religious people, that AIDS and homosexuality are and will always be one and the same, and that we are promiscuous and diseased creatures. That would be repulsive and immoral. I reject, as must any decent person, all the religious and cultural representations of AIDS that associate it with either divine retribution or end-of-millennium crisis. I reject "the metaphors of AIDS," to echo Susan Sontag.[16]

AIDS stands as a symbol—our symbol—because, in its unprecedented impact on our lives, it has taught us so much about ourselves as human beings and as gay men, and because it continues to circumscribe how we choose to live today. Nothing has been the same for us since the advent of AIDS, and nothing will be the same in the future, at least until either a vaccine or a cure is discovered. AIDS has forced us to make all sorts of moral and ethical choices we never really had to consider, in the only context in which such choices make sense, that of another human person. It has altered our sexual behavior in important ways, though the long-term impact remains uncertain. It has given us a new and much refined perspective on relationships and on the meaning of commitment. It has uncovered some fairly amazing things about us: we can be caring, and gentle, and good, and decent. And it has reminded us, in rather painful ways we would not choose if we could, of the persistent and compelling human need for transcendence and meaning, and of the importance of spirituality to our overall health. The tragedy of AIDS has matured us, not excessively I would like to believe, but just enough to impart a measure of wisdom to our lives. It symbolizes, in sum, our adulthood.

Our relationships and our sexuality: these are the opposing poles, the symbols of our individual and collective existence in these uncertain and fragile times, as they have been at all times. The first represents a pull toward integration; the second, an equally strong one toward resistance. The one reaffirms our common membership in the human family; the other has the creative potential to differentiate us from it. Our personal experience tells us that we often waver between the two: craving one, yet desiring the other. We want marriage, and family, and lover; we equally want, more often than we are sometimes prepared to admit, anonymous tricks and pickups, and the uncertain grope in the back room. Many of us spend our lives negotiating delicately between these two extremes. There is nothing wrong about this. It is what ethical human choices are all about.

Let me briefly recount the story of a friendship. I met this friend many years ago, at the exact time that I had broken up with my first lover. I was in a bar, hoping to ease the pain of the parting in the time-honored fashion of drinking to excess and then falling into someone else's arms. I remember my friend's pickup line: "I'm not sure if it's me, but everyone here seems to be part of a couple." Undoubtedly hackneyed, yet also very perceptive. I, for one, was not part of a couple anymore. We went to his place. After a few obligatory and unsatisfactory couplings, the relationship developed into a close friendship. He was good for me. He kept me sane during those months of my breakup.

I always admired him, as I still do, for one "quality" that I do not seem to possess: his remarkable and endearing ability to engage in all manner of sexual activity without indulging in useless guilt. We have always shared a strong complicity, despite the turns and inevitable distance that have grown between us in recent years. I believe that we develop close relationships and friendships for a reason, very often because we need to be taught one of life's important lessons. In the case of my friend, one of these lessons had to do with the need to accept and celebrate gay sexuality fully. In the early years of our friendship, I envied his defiance of sexual norms, his flair for the sexually unorthodox. We were opposites: I, the one needing stability and relationships; he, the more adventurous one. We embodied the inherent polarities of gay life today.

One of the remarkable qualities of any form of spirituality is its inherent ability to move beyond opposites; to achieve integration, not in spite of such opposites, but precisely through and because of them. As human beings, we make ethical choices in much the same way. Our choices are never really pure or totally disinterested. We work with the material facts that are at our disposal and that constitute the tapestry of our lives. These choices become our stories and our symbols. They engender the myths that transform our lives and help us touch the eternal in ourselves and in others.

The rainbow flag, a fairly universal symbol of gay pride, consists of six equal bands of color, each color representing an aspect of what it means to be gay: red, light; orange, healing; yellow, sun; green, harmony with nature; blue, art; and purple, spirit. At one point, there were extra bands, one of which was black, presumably in recognition of what AIDS was doing to our community. Anecdote has it that it was removed when the colors were fixed, so as not to imply that AIDS was to be with us forever. The color purple, representing spirit, was retained. It strikes me as particularly revealing and hopeful that this flag, which has emerged as our *one* genuine symbol worldwide, should include a reference to the important role of spirituality in our lives. In choosing the purple over the black—the transcendent over the merely transitory—we have chosen life over death, and we have reaffirmed spirit over matter.

# 5

# Rituals: Sexual and Otherwise

I OFFER THREE STORIES in tandem, three snapshots in time. The first is a paschal reflection, linked to the arrival of spring and to the apex of the Roman Catholic liturgical year. The second and third are very much contemporary, reflecting the peculiarity and novelty of these anxious times. They have this in common: they bespeak the rites that gay men create for themselves, the passages they are required to undergo, the spaces they choose to inhabit. They are partly fictional, partly real. They are the stories of my life, our lives, and the lives of the many who will come after.

Scene one. New York City. Easter 1978. I have one close friend left from my days in the seminary, and he lives here. As I like to do every Easter, I come to visit. We cherish these days together. We speak about them often, smiling as we recall the ways in which we live at the extremes during these four or five intensely meaningful days. After Holy Thursday service, we have dinner in the Village, and then we hit the bars. We will do this every night, before or after religious services, mixing "the sacred" and "the profane" indiscriminately and rather selectively. There are no contradictions here for us. There is only consistency, and a natural and seamless flow of experience. On Saturday night, before the Easter sunrise service, we spend several hours—considerably longer than we should—in one of those sex bars that the City was so famous for before the arrival of AIDS. This is a new experience for me, an encounter with something dark, and primeval, and terribly attractive. In my voyeuristic mode, I watch from the sidelines, agog with amazement and wonder. I am surrounded by the strength and raw desire of masculine beauty. Andrew Sullivan speaks of sexual experience as "almost a sacrament of human existence."[1] As I ascend from the gloom of the bar into the freshness of early dawn on this Easter Sunday morning, I am renewed and reborn in my identity as a gay man. The intensity of what I have witnessed and, yes, experienced is as holy to me as the holiest of Catholic rites. The sacrament of the risen Lord that I am about to celebrate will resonate as deeply within me as did the ecstatic look on the faces of the men I have regrettably and only temporarily left behind.

Scene two. Montreal. 1998. Some twenty years later. I have asked to be tested for the HIV virus. Reluctantly, because he does not believe it to be warranted, my doctor agrees. I know there is no serious reason for me to take the test or to be concerned about its results. The wait is only three days. Yet in my unfounded and irrational fears about a potentially positive result, I transform this brief period of time into a living hell. In my mind, I go over every detail of every apocalyptic scenario I can imagine. The day comes for the return visit, and I drag my lover with me to the doctor's office, fearful of my reaction should the results prove to be positive. They are not. The sigh of relief is palpable, to the point that tears of relief well up. I have undergone an experience that gay men like me all over the world have to confront every day, and for whom the outcomes are far more devastating than they were for me. This is, in many ways, the quintessentially postmodern "rite of passage," an increasingly formative moment for gay men today.

Scene three. Montreal. Same year. The Black and Blue Ball, one of the top five circuit parties in the world. Primarily because I have never attended one, and partly out of intellectual curiosity, I decide I need to go this year. It is a mammoth event, and the attendance reaches into the thousands. As I enter the large, garagelike space where it is held, the floor vibrates with the unceasing beat of techno dance music. I have not taken the drugs that are so much a part of all such events because I do not want to, but also because I want to observe this celebrated ritual of contemporary gay life from a somewhat balanced and sober perspective. I am, quite literally, bowled over. I have never experienced anything like it before. The bodies of the shirtless men dancing are sculpted, beautiful, and sweaty. The huge crowd stirs as one large, ever moving creature with a mind and a discipline all its own. The music reaches a feverish pitch, the lights and the smoke cast an otherworldly glow over the whole scene, and the dancers yell and meld with one voice. I climb high into the bleachers, looking down on a fabulous scene of orgiastic delight and intensity. I also spend a fair amount of time walking around the perimeter of the inner sanctum that is the dance floor. It is all carefully orchestrated. It is big business. There is another equally interesting, though somewhat irritating, aspect to the party. It is attended by obviously straight adolescents of both sexes. I am protective of my spaces and my environment as a gay man. I just do not like the fact that these "kids" have invaded them. Nonetheless, this dance, as with all the others that are part of "the circuit" the world over, is the closest many gay men will ever come to a form of religious experience. Standing there, I can understand why.

These three "moments" reveal something important about the shape of gay lives today: they are and can be highly ritualized. Most human activity is ritualized activity. Whether it is something as simple or ordinary as observing table manners or shaking hands, or something far more elaborate and extraordinary such as marriage or funerary arrangements, our lives are circumscribed by a complex array of codes and prohibitions that determine the nature and the quality of our interactions. Apart from its regulatory functions, ritual imparts meaning and sense to our many activities. It conditions and provides a context for our responses to life's unexpected and difficult transitions. Much ritual has a strong religious flavor to it, essentially because much human activity takes its inspiration from, and is grounded in, religious activity.

Let us return to my three stories. The first brings together sex and religion rather explicitly. It draws a parallel between sex as a sacramental act—as something signifying sacred power—and the formal liturgy of the Catholic Church. I recall that there was no difference between the two levels of experience; one easily melted into the other. Both were occasions for celebration. Somehow, the religious intensity of these three days merged effortlessly with the equally strong erotic intensity of the sex club. In a significant way, both were affirmations of unbridled life and energy. In one case, it was the victory of life over death as expressed in the person of the risen Christ; in the other, it was the possibility of human touch and human contact through the most life-affirming human act. I also think something even more primal was at work. I believe my friend and I were unconsciously tapping in to an elemental fact of human experience: the erotic and the religious are, at heart, one and the same force. Easter is, after all, the Christian remembrance of ancient fertility rites celebrating the arrival of spring and the awakening of nature. We were reliving this motif in a very direct and intimate way. And we were reliving it as only gay men could, by celebrating the sexual potency of other men.

The second story is about a different and rather unique ritual, one that has been traditionally referred to in the scholarly literature as "a rite of passage."[2] Rites of passage are rituals that mark the transitions from one identity to another. They have generally been understood as consisting of three distinct yet interrelated stages or moments: separation, liminality, and reintegration. Most often, they are associated with the passage from childhood to adulthood, though they can also mark changes in one's social or economic status. Rites of passage are heavily conditioned by the particular culture in which they find themselves, and they are revealing indicators of the culture. For many gay men today, being tested for the HIV virus is a significant and very difficult rite of passage. After coming out, it is perhaps the one defining moment in the formation of the contemporary gay identity. There are several aspects of this experience to consider. The first is that the very fact of undergoing, or having to undergo, the test places you in a different group of people from the average, hence the separation. Taking the test says something unequivocal about your sexual practices and perhaps also about your sexual orientation. In addition, the acute psychological angst associated with such feelings as guilt or uncertainty only heightens the feeling of separation. The phase of liminality or indetermination, when a new identity or status is in the process of being formed, corresponds to the waiting time. In most cases, this will stretch out to several weeks. It is a time of intense vulnerability and insecurity, when you review every real or imaginary implication of a positive result. I recall my great fear of how a positive result would radically alter my life, and how it would force me to make choices I would not have to confront in the normal course of events. Finally, there are the results. Positive or negative, they are the context and the occasion for a sudden reintegration of the self into the habitual patterns of existence. Interestingly enough, the outcome is almost a secondary consideration, even though a positive one would imply an abrupt and irreversible shift in identity. What is important is the fact of having been tested. Afterward, you are never quite the same person.

Anyone struggling with a potentially fatal disease, whether it is cancer or the like, will undergo a similar metamorphosis. At a fundamental level, therefore, there is nothing particularly unique about being tested for HIV versus being tested for any other serious health condition. What makes the critical difference, however, is the stigma attached to HIV and to AIDS. In itself, this is so powerful that the person undergoing the test cannot help being influenced by it. Hence, in large part, the reason for the guilt, and the anxiety, and the depression, and the very real fear. Though the HIV test may well be a contemporary rite of passage for many gay men, it remains a ritual fraught with danger. This danger does not stem from the gay condition itself; rather, it emerges from the considerably more burdensome one produced by social ostracism and jeopardy.

Our third snapshot in time is celebratory and joyful. The mega-events that are gay circuit parties have elicited a considerable amount of attention from all quarters and all types of writers, gay and straight. The most recent is Michelangelo Signorile, whose bestselling book, *Life Outside*, casts a somewhat jaundiced and moralistic eye on the excesses associated with these parties.[3] The trouble with Signorile is that he all too easily and quite clumsily proposes a religious analysis of circuit parties, as though they could best be understood as a form of sectarian behavior. Such a facile approach, while perhaps more readily marketable, ultimately fails to provide a convincing explanation for this phenomenon from a properly nuanced and balanced perspective. Other analysts, though also using a religious frame of reference, are far more refined and cautious in their approach.[4]

It is perhaps fair to claim that the circuit party phenomenon would not have existed had it not been for AIDS. These events are big fund-raisers for a variety of AIDS-related charities. Beyond this rational, formal explanation, however, there lies a more profound, seemingly irrational one. Circuit parties are a grandiose, very dramatic, and very public affirmation of the resiliency of life in the face of overwhelming loss and devastation. They provide an escape valve, a way of remembering those who have gone, while at the same time reminding those left behind that life is indeed more powerful than death. They also hearken back to the pre-AIDS era of Dionysian release and excess, when dancing, drugs, and sex provided the focus for so much of gay life. While undoubtedly elitist, they remain a vibrant affirmation of tribal kinship and oneness, and of the amazing strength of the gay community today.

In some important ways, circuit parties have many qualities of the primitive religious experience of worship.[5] Emile Durkheim has remarked on how religious feeling—the sacred—emerges in the context of social environments characterized by their effervescence. The circuit party has been described as "the queer liturgical rite" and "the public worship of homosex." Dancing, music, and mind-altering substances (whether alcohol or drugs) are instrumental in creating a particular mood and milieu, as might be the case in certain tribal contexts. The dancers "call upon the ancient ways of celebrating oneness," and through fan-dancing, they are "calling up the spirits," offering "a memorial of those who have died." It is "the ritual that creates community," a time and a place standing slightly outside the mundane and the ordinary, yet radically transgressive of them. The circuit party infringes upon religious worship, in that "male beauty [is seen] as the god that requires worship." Even the space it occupies is religious. There are an inner sanctum (the dance floor) and an outer one (its periphery). There is the holy of holies, the DJ's booth, "where the high priest intercedes" on behalf of the dancing worshipers. Moreover, like all liturgical forms, the circuit party creates "a separate enclave of meaning" where certain values—values unique to the tribe—are staged and re-affirmed. The existence of a universal network of circuit parties frequented by a core nucleus of gay men has interesting parallels with the phenomenon of the religious pilgrimage.[6]

These three examples of gay rituals lead us to consider the broader question of the religious dimensions of certain aspects of the contemporary gay experience. We will briefly examine four of these: sexuality and eroticism, activism, physical enclaves, and last but by no means least, coming out.

## Holy Sex

A close friend—I shall call him Daniel—is a fan of male strip joints. He goes to these clubs once or twice per week, on average. He often discusses his experiences with me, describing how the strippers flirt with the customers, and how the ritual of the back-room lap dance unfolds. Daniel has lost his heart more often than he cares to remember to the boyish charms of these dancers. In his more sober moments, he reflects on the power dynamics inherent in these encounters, power dynamics based on the exchange of money for sex, of fleeting physical contact for companionship. Daniel has remarked over the years on the stories that many of the dancers have recounted to him, stories of missing fathers, of substance abuse of various sorts, and of their need to find the perfect, kind client who will take care of them. He is very much the fatherly type, mature and well established. "No wonder they like him," I tell myself, not without a hint of sarcasm.

At times, Daniel describes his encounters in the strip joints in religious terms. Partly, he does this, I am sure, out of a measure of affectionate teasing toward me. Yet he can be serious and eloquent about the "hallowed" nature of the close interactions between himself and the dancers, and about the highly ritualized environment that regulates them. This is similar to another friend, Robert, who is on the fringes of the gay sadomasochistic scene. Robert has been into S/M for as long as I have known him. A tall, handsome man, he is always "the top" or "the master" in his sexual exchanges. Robert uses some of the same language as Daniel when talking about his activities, words such as "trust," "power," "limits," "care," "vulnerability," and "surpass." In Robert's descriptions of what he does, I am always struck by the complexity of the codes and the customs regulating S/M sex, but more particularly by the implicit trust and vulnerability that the two (or more) partners must ceaselessly demonstrate toward each other. Perhaps nowhere else in gay culture can one find such a symbolically charged and almost mystical form of erotic behavior. Yet it continues to be scoffed at and denigrated as something marginal and repulsive. In his incisive study of the gay leather scene, Geoff Mains touches on the element of trust: "In their commitment to one another, humans have a strong need to put their lives symbolically on the line. Doing so is a path toward self-definition. Leather play is a form of that process, and the fraternal and trusting atmosphere that exists between its players makes it all the more possible and all the more rewarding."[7]

I ask myself if Daniel and Robert are not a bit too romantic or too naive in their approach to gay erotic play as a form of religious or spiritual illumination. The idea that the erotic can be the occasion for an expression of, and for an encounter with, the holy or the transcendent is common to most religions. Yet what about gay sex in particular makes it different in this regard, if at all? Is it really appropriate to talk about "holy sex," as though gay sexual activity were qualitatively better or superior to other forms of erotic expression? Is there something unique or generic to same-sex erotic relations that can give us a privileged glimpse of the greater divine purpose or that can at least make us question our sexual assumptions?

An argument was made in an earlier chapter concerning the special "vocation" of homosexuals—that, by virtue of our marginality, we call into question many generally accepted societal norms, particularly those having to do with fixed gender identity and gender relations. Even though Americanized commercial gay culture is not, at first glance, as cutting-edge as might be desirable, the fact remains that gay men stand as a stark reminder to the wider heterosexual culture of its contingency and indeterminacy. That is why straight society, although it may be prepared to "grant us" certain rights (privileges in the eyes of some), does not want to hear about what we do in bed, where, with whom, and certainly not how often. Hence the oft-repeated question: "Why must you flaunt it so much?" As though all the glossy, sexualized, and straight commercialism thrown at us on a daily basis is not "flaunting it."

Gay sexual activity is not qualitatively better or superior to other forms of erotic expression. It is, however, discrepant and anarchistic, and therein lies the special quality that makes it so fundamentally different. It has always been, it remains, and it will undoubtedly always be uncontrolled and uncontrollable by the guardians of the so-called public morality. Even if it becomes sanctioned by marriage or another form of public commitment, there will still be a faint smell of the illegal and the sinful about it. Many believe that this is good and necessary. To remain healthy, society needs those who stand at its margins, the better to judge it and, in so doing, to edge it forward.

Though all sexual relations are founded on the dynamic of power, the fact that gay erotic relations are between persons of the same sex necessarily ensures a more balanced and even distribution of this power. One finds, in same-sex relations, a mutuality and an implicit level of understanding that make the communication vital to a relationship easier and, in a way, more immediately accessible. Moreover, same-sex erotic relations can be an occasion for the explicit enunciation of power, for its staging and acting out, and for its eventual subversion. This is what Robert's S/M escapades are about, as are, to a lesser degree, the experiences of Daniel. Both are part of a dynamic of mutuality and subversion. They call into question accepted patterns of role differentiation, and they do so not by ignoring this difference, but by exaggerating its claims to normalcy. If you can play "at" or "with" something, you necessarily undermine its power, good or bad, over you. Gay camp and cross-dressing perform a similarly critical and much-needed role.

"Holy sex" could imply any number of things. It could refer to sexual activity to serve religious or ritualistic purposes, or to please or honor the deity. Examples might be ancient temple prostitution or the orgiastic excesses of certain fertility rites. It could also be a form of ascetic or mystical discipline, a demanding path to enlightenment as that found in certain esoteric traditions of the East and the West. A third, more prosaic meaning has to do with its opposite: sexual nonindulgence as a means to spiritual illumination. In this case, sex becomes "holy" by virtue of its being controlled for a higher purpose.

When my friends Daniel and Robert, or other gay friends and acquaintances, indulge in sexual activity, they are engaging in an act of worship. In this case, both a person and an elemental force of nature are worshiped. The person is masculine; the force is masculinity. Anyone who has ever publicly cruised other men, or participated in some of the more arcane rituals associated with S/M sex, for example, will understand the powerful, almost overwhelming pull of the masculine and the unspoken codes with which we surround and protect it. Masculinity represents many things for gay men: potency, dominion, authority, abandonment, protection. As the dominant masculine symbol, the phallus acquires many characteristics of the holy. This is not a particularly modern interpretation. Phallic worship is as old as human civilization, and perhaps as controversial today as it was in the past. It has always been transgressive, associated with disorder and excess, with riotous freedom and wanton sex. Keith Haring, the young gay graffiti artist who died of complications from AIDS in 1990, well understood the power of the phallus. In his early work, he often portrayed it with a halo around its tip, being worshiped by erect male attendants.[8] I call gay sex "holy sex" because it is centered on one of the primal symbols of the natural world, that of male regenerative power. The rites of gay sex call forth and celebrate this power, particularly in its unknown and unknowable anonymity. Gay men are the worshipers paying homage to the god who stands erect and omnific, ever silent and distant.

No doubt society cannot stand to be reminded of this, though one would think that its patriarchal nature is such that it might demonstrate more leniency. The problem lies not in a lack of understanding, but in understanding only too well the dangerous nature of what gay men do when they have sex with other men. Gay sex unmasks and subverts masculine power by sacralizing it. It makes this power extraordinary rather than ordinary, sacred rather than mundane, holy rather than temporal. It messes up the boundaries of what appears fixed, taken for granted, and too ordinary, what is presumed to be natural and orderly, by placing it on a higher and more distant symbolic plane where it necessarily and properly belongs. In so doing, gay men reveal phallic power to be sacred power, not the power of everyday oppression. And there is nothing messier or more disturbing than the holy when it decides to reveal itself and to intervene in the smugness of human affairs.

## The Liturgy of Activism

Gay liberation and the AIDS crisis have one point in common: both have given rise to important forms of political activism. Much of this activism has been fueled by anger and frustration as well as by a genuine commitment to issues of nondiscrimination and human rights. We have marched and sat in, demonstrated and yelled, volunteered and chained ourselves to fences. We have signed petitions and raised money, accompanied the dying and fought for medication, protested, held vigils, and even thrown the occasional pavement stone. We took on the psychiatrists and lived to talk about it. Some of us have been consumed with "fighting the good fight" in the public arena, while others have retreated silently into the anonymity and comfort of our checkbooks. We have been brave and eloquent, stupid and silent, creative and mainstream. We have given birth to engaged forms of public art, and we have literally invented new forms of health activism. We have written about our lives and our times, mourned our dead warriors, and inspired the mounting generation. We have done all this for a good and noble cause, for our survival as a people. We have been the most excessive and committed of believers.

Political engagement can serve many functions in the lives of individuals, as it can in the lives of communities. It provides focus and meaning, sometimes allowing us to work through a crisis or a deeper unresolved issue. It offers an outlet for our idealism and altruism, and it gives flesh to our beliefs. One of its more important roles is its expression of human solidarity and compassion. The gay response to the AIDS crisis has been eloquent in this regard, and some scholars have remarked on the close parallels between AIDS volunteerism and religious sentiment.[9] Of course, most visibly and most fundamentally, political activism effects change. Though this may often be more a hope than a reality, it constitutes the driving force behind all others.

Gay political activism has been successful in implementing its agenda of change. In the earliest post-Stonewall days of the movement, it was instrumental in bringing homosexuality into the public consciousness of Americans, and in leading the battle to have it removed from the official listing of mental disorders.[10] There then came the campaigns against ex–beauty queen Anita Bryant[11] and the various state and municipal ballot and ordinance initiatives seeking to limit gay rights. In the United States, the gay movement has had to contend with the continued and well-orchestrated public animosity generated by the Religious Right. The biggest battle has been AIDS. Gay activists were, and continue to be, in the forefront of the fight for proper care and more democratic and open access to testing and medication. More recently, the energy has shifted to such issues as the military, marriage, and public and private benefits plans. Different countries, because they are culturally unique, generate different issues, and it would be inappropriate to assume that U.S. gay activism sets the universal activist agenda, though it undoubtedly remains influential well beyond its immediate national borders. In Canada, for example, much of the struggle for gay rights has taken place in the context of modifications to federal and provincial human rights legislation, and often the governments themselves have taken the initiative in ensuring their inclusion.[12]

As with much of what human beings do, political activism can be a form of religious or quasi-religious activity. The passion and energy with which it is embarked upon, the idealism and the quest for the common good sustaining it, the desire to help others that nourishes it, the belief in a higher purpose that maintains the commitment—all these are qualities one might find in the true religious believer. The faith of the truly engaged and committed political activist is different from that of the religious person *not* in the degree of its intensity or passion, but in its object-choice. Where the former may limit this choice to very precise and exacting strategies for change, the latter opts for a more amorphous and universal set of symbolic tools.

A ritual flow to political activism that makes it almost liturgical in form is particularly the case for AIDS activism. Liturgical rites are condensed enclaves of religious meaning, where an intensity of feeling is achieved through the repeated and stylized use of symbols, sound, and movement. The intent is to attain a type of stasis, where time and space are transformed into more meaningful dimensions of existence. AIDS activism has always been seen as performance. This stems, in large measure, from the queer approach to political action as a vehicle for the deployment of power relations. Liturgy is also performance, and it deals with the staging of sacred power. In analyzing the actions or performances of AIDS activists, one cannot help being struck—even impressed—by their religious and liturgical elements. First, there is the context. This is a life-and-death struggle, and it is being done for dead or dying companions. The performance takes on the shape of a requiem, a memorial. Second, there are the symbols: the red ribbon, the Silence = Death pink triangle logo, the blood as both sign of life and potential threat. These symbols, and others like them, provide visual focus and energy for the struggle. Third, the mood of the event, while certainly defiant, remains marked by an element of theatricality and even, at times, solemnity. The shouting of slogans is important, but so is a respectful and caring silence. These are only some of the interesting parallels. In their passion and grandeur, these actions recall and repeat religious and liturgical paradigms.

I will never forget the first time I saw some panels from the AIDS quilt. It was on the occasion of the Montreal International AIDS Conference. I have seen many parts of it since then, and my reaction has invariably been the same. I am moved and also angry. I would think that most gay men probably respond in a similar way. As beautiful and touching as the quilt may be, it stands as a stark reminder of the desperation and suffering caused by this epidemic, and of the criminal neglect that marked its early years. To this day, whenever I see panels from the quilt, I am equally fearful—fearful that I may recognize the name of someone and that my grief will be without end.

The AIDS quilt has emerged as one of the most powerful and enduring symbols of the pandemic, but also as one of the most religious, if not the only truly religious one. There are obvious reasons. Above all else, the quilt is a memorial, a large, movable gravestone. Because it represents the most explicit association of the pandemic with death, more precisely with the deaths of certain individuals, it naturally elicits the feelings of awe and respect that all such funerary symbols evoke. When we think of death, we tend to ponder inherently religious questions. The quilt, moreover, puts us face-to-face with our own mortality and does so quite painfully if we are HIV positive or if we have developed AIDS. It places us in a long line of others who have had to deal with this condition, and therefore offers support and solidarity in the face of human finiteness and suffering. The quilt provides space and time for mourning. It creates the conditions necessary for the expression of our grief, and thereby for its eventual integration into our lives. It is a redemptive, regenerative symbol, one that, in remembering, also heals.

The rituals surrounding the AIDS quilt are highly liturgical in form and content. This point has been picked up by a number of writers, who remark, at times with incredulity, on this strange phenomenon.[13] There is nothing strange or unusual about it. It reminds us, once again, of the necessary place of ritual in our lives. Anyone who has witnessed the ceremony marking the unfurling of the panels for public display, or who has seen it on film, will instantly be reminded of the highly structured, solemn flow of the ceremonial. The opening and rotation of the sets of panels one by one, the helpers clad only in white, the momentous litany of names, the silence hovering over the entire affair—these are elements of liturgy. As with all liturgy, this ceremony creates "a separate enclave of meaning," a space and a time standing *outside* space and time, a moment of eternity in the here and now. Historically, the AIDS quilt emerged from AIDS political activism. Interestingly enough, though, it has come to symbolize the very soul of the pandemic, its spiritual articulation. It may yet turn out to be activism's one lasting legacy.

## SACRED SPACE

Geography can be holy. One need only think of the physical sites sacred to humankind's religions, the sanctuaries and churches dotting our landscape, or the cities such as Jerusalem, Mecca, and Rome that are, for some religious believers, the absolute center of the universe. We live in space; we move in it; we build in it; we leave it as a legacy to our children and to our children's children. In his discussion of the religious sentiments of so-called primitive man, found in his classic work on the nature of religion, *The Sacred and the Profane*, Mircea Eliade talks about the sacred "breaking through" time in order to found a holy place, a sacred space.[14] This space becomes the center of the world, the axis around which all else revolves. Very often, it is associated with home and hearth, a human concept to which we—even though we may be thoroughly modern, atomized individuals—can still instinctively and passionately resonate. Sacred space can also be forbidden space, circumscribed by prohibitions and taboos designed to contain its power and prevent it from seeping into and inhabiting the realm of the profane.

We create our own sacred spaces. All of us have these places, even if they are only in our minds, to which we retreat, and from which we gather strength and resiliency to confront the harshness of daily existence. Communities also have these places. They are sometimes associated with history, very often with its formative or tragic episodes. On a more mundane level, they can be community gathering places, neighborhoods, or enclaves that sustain identity and nurture the bonds of a fragile unity. They can be the result of a voluntary association or, as in the case of ghettos, savagely and deliberately imposed for reasons of state. Invariably, such spaces denote separateness. This can be highly desirable, or it can imply radical and permanent ostracism. Its positive side has to do with protection and vulnerability, and with the creation of human solidarity; its darker side mirrors the pangs of exclusion and prohibition, and the barbaric unpredictability of human scapegoating.

In my life, I can recall a number of occasions when an encounter with space has assumed religious or spiritual significance. I have already referred to my visit of the Dachau concentration camp near Munich. On the same trip, I sojourned in Rome. For a Catholic, the first time one enters St. Peter's Basilica in the Vatican is a moving and emotionally charged experience. It was for me, and it became acutely so when I knelt in front of the tomb of Pope John XXIII in the crypt under the main altar and tears welled up uncontrollably. Years later, while visiting the south of France, we stopped briefly in the little Alpine town of La Mure, the birthplace of the founder of the religious order to which I had belonged in my younger days. I walked around and visited the various sites associated with his life and death in a paradoxical spirit of contemplative excitement. Though these are all places connected explicitly with religious sentiment, other, considerably more worldly locales have moved me equally. My return visit to my childhood home was one such experience, as was the one to the place where I had spent my novitiate years. Because I am a gay man, my first time in a gay bar, my first visit to the baths, and most poignantly, the first time I stepped into the Stonewall Inn in New York City have also been uplifting, spiritual moments in my life. Part of it is attributable to past memories and to the rites of passage that are the building blocks of everyone's life. But another, deeper part has to do with our visceral need to construct places in our lives where we can encounter what is transcendent and eternal, and where we can be fully authentic selves.

Urban gay enclaves, though they have played an essential role in the emergence of the contemporary North American gay identity,[15] are often derided as self-imposed gay ghettos. Usually, gay men themselves raise this brazen cry. They object to the apparently closed atmosphere of these places, where one meets only other gay men, often the same ones, and where life and its multiple interactions appear hermetic and circular. "Everyone ends up sleeping with everyone else," they will say, not without a touch of envy in their voices. There is nothing quite like meeting former lovers in public places to give one a jaundiced view of the gay world and its inhabitants!

Reality is much more complex and subtle, and thankfully so. Although many aspects of urban gay life can be the target of legitimate criticism, whatever its source, a great deal is positive and affirming about it. Urban gay enclaves can represent any number of important accomplishments: economic clout, political influence, social acceptance, cultural dynamism, urban renewal. Their wide spectrum of institutions and services, many of which were founded *by* gay men *for* gay men, create strong and vibrant centers of public affirmation and collective empowerment. They were and continue to be as critical to our tenacious survival as a community as are the individually courageous, though isolated, acts of coming out. They make a most significant statement: we are here to stay. In doing so, they offer a context for thinking about the future, a measure of hope and meaning. More important, they construct a safe space, where being gay means essentially to be the one defining the norms. This is no mean accomplishment when we consider the norms in effect outside the invisible walls of "the ghetto." In the process of creating these gay enclaves, we consciously exclude. We set ourselves and our brothers "apart," but we do so not because of spite or a sense of arrogance. Rather, we do so because our space is our power, and we need to be able to control and articulate it on our own terms, as peoples and communities have always done down through history.

There is another important way by which gay men create sacred space: through the reappropriation of public space for sexual encounters. By eroticizing ordinary, everyday spaces, gay men provide them with a novel symbolic meaning, one that, while remaining hidden to prying eyes, manages to create sites of alternative sexual expression and resistance. The family park by day becomes the gay hunting ground by night, thereby reversing the "normal," ordinary schema of things. This space is not what it appears to be. There is latent subversive potential to this process. Quite apart from the sheer erotic electricity often found in such spaces, they stand as "open" territory, places of potency and uncertainty. No doubt danger plays a part in this. Equally important, however, the cover of night allows for the emergence of a sense of mythical time and space where everything and anything can be created anew through the simple yet disturbing touch of the unknown.

Gay enclaves and the institutions and spaces that populate them—gay bars and discos, gay baths, gay restaurants and coffeehouses, gay businesses and churches—are the spiritual centers, the sacred loci of the gay community. We draw sustenance and reassurance from them. They allow us to be fully human on our own terms, and thus contribute immensely to our growth and development as a community. They perform an equally important role as sites of transgression and celebration. A perfect example is the spectacle that unfolds in gay neighborhoods everywhere at Halloween. Not only has the feast been reclaimed by gays, but the spirit and life that animate the streets of our ghettos on October 31 are unparalleled anywhere, boldly upsetting everyday notions of propriety and decency.

Whenever I walk down the streets of Montreal's gay "Village," as it is known, I feel pride and affirmation, because my people come to work and play here. They come to cruise, to meet, to worship, and to remember their dead here. It is a place of power and hope. It is sacred space for me and my own, a place where I know I belong—indeed, where I choose to belong.

## THE RITUAL OF RITUALS

Some coming out stories can be wrenchingly sad, while others can be quite amusing. Mine, I would like to think, is a funnier one. If not funny, then perhaps it is one of the more bizarre because of the context in which it took place.

For me, coming out meant coming out to my father more than it did to the rest of the world. Gay sons have always had an ambivalent relationship with their fathers, and I was no exception. I felt an unconscious pressure to succeed for my father so that he could be proud of me. Though we had never spoken about it, he knew what and who I was. Though he had met former boyfriends and lovers, I had never said the words.

The context was a family Christmas gathering where much wine was imbibed, including by me. As is his wont when he does not want to confront issues head-on, my father had been teasing me, asking leading questions. I will admit that I was quite drunk, so I either ignored him or teased back. Later in the evening, as we were playing cards, my father made another loaded remark, and one of my sisters, in a fit of exasperation, blurted out the classic words, "Enough already, he likes men!" Everyone laughed. She had outed me. I finally told my father that yes, I was gay. At that precise moment, I felt a wave of nausea hit me, and I rushed to the kitchen sink, where it all "came out," so to speak. I have always thought that was very symbolic of what had just happened, as though I needed literally to vomit the truth. In the process, I did serious damage to my sister's kitchen plumbing, and she was the one who had told my father what I was. It seems that I was also intent on revenge.

Coming out is really the gay equivalent of coming of age, whatever the number of years one may have attained. Gay authors have written much about it and celebrated it.[16] It is the one defining moment in the lives of gay men. Heterosexual men do not have an equivalent experience because there never is a need for them to decide whether or not to declare themselves to be heterosexuals. They just are, and everything and everyone around them upholds this unmistakable fact of nature, expecting them to behave accordingly and making the necessary allowances when they do. There are rites of passage for heterosexual men in our culture, marking their transition through adolescence into adulthood. These often center on elements of peer acceptance and sexual initiation. But such rites or "moments" are seldom, if ever, associated with painful self-acceptance or with possible rejection by either family or friends. Coming out for a gay youth can and does carry these implications, at times irreversibly so. It can signify exclusion and ridicule, just as it can place one in jeopardy or at risk. At its most extreme, it can lead to self-hatred and to suicide. Coming out is risky business.

Once the risk is assumed, however, the benefits can be and are quite extraordinary. There is a sense of liberation and honesty about one's life and one's relationships. One no longer feels the need or the shame in hiding and denying an important aspect of one's life. One feels stronger and more confident, less vulnerable to uncertainty and to doubt. Interestingly enough, the anxiety one may have experienced about coming out and what this may mean in terms of how one is perceived or treated by others seems to dissipate. It is almost as though one has reintegrated the human family and can now take the place and assume the proper role that have always been one's destiny.

All this sounds rather rosy and romantic, and perhaps it is. There can be little doubt that individual experiences of coming out are far more complex and unpredictable in their results. For some, as is probably the case for all of us, coming out is never a done deal. We spend our entire lives coming out in different situations, always having, or being forced, to correct the world's assumptions about us and those we choose to love. John J. McNeill, for example, writes about coming out as a three-stage process.[17] He describes the first "passage" as self-acceptance, the second as entering into an intimate relation with another person, and the third as the public statement of identity and faith. For some, coming out can be a one-time event, where these various "passages" are rolled into one; for others, however, it is a never-ending struggle. But for all, it is a necessary and vital step on the road to being fully human. Coming out is *the* ritual of the rituals of our lives.

The perceptive reader will have picked up on interesting parallels between coming out and the religious, notably Christian, experience of being "born again." This theme has been noted by others.[18] Both sets of experiences involve a public declaration of identity: for the born-again Christian, that of being a follower of Jesus Christ; for the person coming out, that of being a homosexual. Both are related to the motif of salvation or redemption in that each hints at a sudden and illuminating change for the better when the necessary existential choice is finally made. For the born-again Christian, accepting the salvation and removal of sins already accomplished by Jesus brings about a radical transformation in one's life, just as accepting one's sexual orientation does for the homosexual. Both, however, are predicated on free choice and on the necessity of using it. If the decision is not made, then there is no liberation from the past, no redemptive grace. And certainly no forgiveness of sins.

Coming out implies separation, and it implies giving up a normative identity for a transgressive one. In biblical language, coming out signifies exile; in the language of psychoanalysis, it intimates mourning. John McNeill writes:

> John Fortunato in his gay spiritual classic *Embracing the Exile: Healing Journeys of Gay Christians* deals with the gay experience of passage under another biblical symbol, that of "Exile." Using this symbol, Fortunato brings out the psychological and spiritual meaning of self-acceptance for gays. Fortunato identifies staying in the closet with the fundamental myth of our culture, the myth that happiness and fulfillment can be achieved by belonging in this world. We lesbians and gays are aware that our very existence as

homosexually oriented persons makes us exiles in our heterosexist culture. If we come out of the closet, we will most frequently have the painful and frightening experience of being exiles from family, friends, church, and culture. We will experience being outsiders who no longer belong.

Consequently, in Fortunato's view, many gay people strive to hide their gay identity, even from themselves, in order to be accepted. The only healthy spiritual way to deal with our exile status is for gay people to go through a process of mourning, gradually letting go of our desire to belong to and be accepted by all the structures of the heterosexist world. At the same time we must deepen our experience of belonging in the spiritual world.[19]

This perspective on the process of coming out is an obviously religious one, but it spells out clearly the implications of the choice and the reality that it reflects. There can be no denying that coming out, while it may open up certain possibilities, implies the rejection of something else that is "normal." This is not always an easy choice to live with, and it is not always successful either. Coming out can be likened to a journey, a pilgrimage of the soul. If it is, in fact, a lifelong struggle with authenticity, and if it is essential to the elaboration of a healthy gay personality, then it can also be said to be a societal as well as a religious necessity. Psychologically well-balanced individuals are the foundation of healthy citizenship and sound belief.

This chapter has proposed a religious reading of aspects of gay life today, particularly from the viewpoint of ritual behavior. I obviously do not mean to suggest that being gay is a religion, even though being more authentically gay could and should lead us to act in more religious, or at least spiritual, ways. I only want to offer a different perspective for understanding our lives as gay men, one that recognizes their ritual dimensions and values their multiple expressions. Spirituality is about integrity and the quest for transcendence. I believe that the rites and passages of our gay lives are genuine attempts at carving places for ourselves in this world, and that when we do this, we stake a claim for those gay men—brothers all—who will come after us. Only by remaining faithful to our future as a community can we act responsibly in the present.

# 6

# The Experience of Wholeness

# in Community

IN THE MID-1970s, at the time when I was struggling with my uncertain sexual identity, I accidentally stumbled upon a book that had just been released in paperback. It is strange how there are key moments in one's life when one recalls everything in acute detail. I remember that I picked it up on a warm spring Sunday evening in a drugstore, near the place where I was living with my girlfriend at that time. When I did so, I felt an unusual tingle, as though something momentous were about to happen. What first struck me about the book was its cover. There was something incredibly Harlequinesque about it, like a steamy pulp novel read by pubescent girls or lonely spinsters. Two men were depicted: a younger, blond one in running shorts and sneakers, sitting with his head turned toward an older man with a towel around his waist, standing behind him. The blurb on the back cover boldly proclaimed the book to be "the first honest popular novel about homosexual love." The book was *The Front Runner* by Patricia Nell Warren, and as stereotypical as it may sound, the book literally changed my life.

I believe in fate, and I believe I was destined to pick up that particular book, on that particular evening, at that particular point in my life. It was "a moment of grace," as a dear friend of mine would say. I paid for the book on the sly, so as not to evoke suspicion. I read it stealthily at home, as though it might disclose some deep, dark secret about my inner soul, and discreetly marked the passages I thought especially beautiful or incisive. Any gay man who was around in the 1970s will recall the power of this book. It is incredibly romantic, and for the first time in popular fiction, it describes homosexual love as something attainable, though unfortunately tragic. A runaway bestseller, it is also a tear-jerker in the truest sense of the word. It tells the story of Billy Sive, a young long-distance runner, and his coach, Harlan Brown, who is an older man. They meet, fall in love, get married, and Billy sires a son with a lesbian friend before being shot dead by a homophobic killer while running the 5,000-meter race at the 1976 Montreal Olympics. In many ways, it is a traditionally "straight" love story, hence the reason, I believe, for its allure. It made the impossible seem very much possible and mainstream for us.

I told everyone about the book and bought copies for all the important people in my life: lovers, friends, the therapist I was seeing at the time. I gave them away as gifts, hoping that they would reveal much about me without my having to verbalize it. The book was a watershed. There is no question that the story line is melodramatic and sentimental, almost corny, and that is exactly what made it so attractive. I had never really considered that love between two men could be a beautiful, romantic thing, and that the commitment it entailed could be as ennobling and uplifting—spiritual, in fact—as that between a man and a woman. For someone on the verge of coming out, who was still involved in a relationship with a woman, such affirmation was important and timely. *The Front Runner* was the beginning of the process of self-acceptance for me because it showed me another way, and it did so through the medium of a simple but effective love story.

A few years later, I discovered my favorite author, Christopher Isherwood. By that time, I was with my first male lover, and I had begun to construct, somewhat gingerly, my gay identity. Anyone familiar with Isherwood's writing will know that he has a rather particular style, which he likens to that of a camera. He is always observing in his novels, trying to catch the exact detail of a figure or a conversation, recording the nuances of context and dialogue. He is best known for his stories of Berlin in the 1930s.[1] As a gay author and a practicing Vedantist, he wrote extensive biographical and semibiographical material, a large part of which explores the never-ending struggle between religious idealism and sexual longing. My encounter with Isherwood's writing was an equally significant affair. Quite apart from his style, which I particularly enjoyed (and still do), his exploration of the complementary themes of religion, politics, and sex struck a chord deep within me, for I was striving to make sense of those elements in my life. In the 1960s, he wrote a small masterpiece of a book, called *A Single Man*, which would deserve to be recognized as one of the literary accomplishments of this century. A remarkable study of solitude and aging, it tells the intimate story of a gay college professor who recently lost his companion, but who manages to live his days (a single day, in this particular case) in quiet but desperate dignity. Isherwood taught me that a gay life could be lived with deliberate passion and commitment. While Warren's book showed me that romantic gay love was attainable, even though it might be fictional, Isherwood sketched out the contours of a meaningful gay existence, one where it was possible to be religious and a homosexual at the same time.

My two stories allude to the transformative power of literature, to how our lives can be shaped and guided by the written word, which engages us at critical moments in our development. Literature, as with any form of cultural expression, is a site of human transcendence. We enter into dialogue with the words and the story, and we allow them to take us out of ourselves, fashioning for us new worlds and new ways of looking at the old, challenging us to adopt a critical stance vis-à-vis our current understanding of reality. When I cried at the story of Billy and Harlan, for example, and even though I knew it was not real, I was imagining and creating for myself an alternate scenario to the standard one of boy-meets-girl. Though it was boy-meets-boy in this case, it was enough to plant in me the conviction that it was what I wanted and what I could and should have. Similarly, when I read the stories of Isherwood's life, as thinly disguised as they were in the trappings of fiction, I knew that the possibilities of an exciting and fully creative gay life were more than just that; they were authentic and justified.

The gay "self" is a self in dialogue. This dialogue takes place in a number of directions at once, but the two most significant arenas are the larger heterosexual world and the more limited, though very influential, gay community. It is in terms of, and in opposition to, the former that gay men most clearly establish *who* we are. It is a definition marked by oppositions: not straight, not paternal, not macho, and so forth. The latter, on the other hand, defines *what* we are. It marks us as part of something larger than our discrete selves. It proclaims to the world that we are gay, and "by the way, have you also noticed that we are proud, and open, and defiant, and will not simply go away?" Gay men continuously negotiate a dialogue, and engage in an uneasy truce, with both of these aspects of our lives. Most of us function, because we have to for professional or other reasons, in the predominantly straight world, and we often play a subtle game of hide-and-seek with it, even though we may be defiantly out. We accept and live with some of the values and expectations of this world. At times, however, we choose to identify ourselves more with the gay world, claiming as our own many of the normative discourses of this community and participating in its rituals and institutions. We may also find the gay world restrictive and closed, too self-contained or self-absorbed. Though we value and cherish it as a "safe space" for us, we sometimes step back from its overpowering and crushing presence.

Let us return to the word "tribe," which we considered earlier. It has emerged in recent years in certain circles as nomenclature for the gay community. The word bothers some people to a great extent. I recall being at lunch with a straight woman friend who became positively hateful when referring to a gay man who used it rather frequently. Though she was generally open-minded about many things, particularly those of a sexual nature, her reaction in this case was totally irrational. Upon reflection, I realized that it disturbed her for two basic reasons: because it implies radical separateness, and therefore the rejection of something, and because it denotes an uncompromising element of superiority or influence. There is also something exotic and mysterious about a tribe. It has the connotation of exciting primitiveness.

"Tribe" contains interesting anthropological and biblical overtones. It also touches upon some of the central themes found in gay life today. From a sociological point of view, "tribe" refers to a form of social organization, usually based on a unity of families claiming a common ancestry. It is generally a self-contained economic unit, where the production of life's necessities is endogenous to the group. In more common parlance, the word is sometimes used in a derogatory sense, implying exclusion and exclusivity, such as when speaking of a closed grouping of professionals or a closely knit family. "Tribe," in any context, invariably signifies closeness, self-dependence, and a measure of distance from other or similar social groupings, yet it can also imply secrecy.

In the context of the Hebrew and Christian Scriptures, the word "tribe" makes one think immediately of the twelve tribes of Israel. The social structure of early Israel was tribal, and each tribe carried the name of an ancestor common to all its members. The twelve tribes became the chosen people, one nation especially selected by God for the purpose of

carrying out the divine plan of redemption. There is a theologically positive connotation to the concept of tribe. By referring directly to the instru-
mentality of salvation, "tribe" is transformed into an important means for
the implication of the holy in the workings of human affairs. It becomes a
site of divine revelation. It is something set apart, chosen for the execution
of a bigger purpose and a consecrated plan.

In referring to the gay community as "our tribe," all of these richly
laden meanings usually associated with the word are retained, yet they are
transformed into something else. "Tribe" signifies an identity that is above
all collective and founded on difference. It implies that all its members
share a common set of characteristics, that of a similar sexual orientation.
In addition, it indicates a nostalgic return to a certain ethnographic or
anthropological primitiveness wherein a particular group of people—in
this case, gay people—can be understood and defined through the unusual
rituals and symbols characterizing them. The lure of the exotic is very
much present here. It functions in the dual and simultaneous sense of affirmation and mystification. On the one hand, it confirms and strengthens
gay identity; on the other, it muddles the precise contours of this identity
from the perspective of the outsider looking in. I would suggest that
"tribe" is a word unconsciously associated with talismanic power. I think
we like to use it in reference to ourselves because it carries overtones of
protection and safety, and it imparts a sense of good fortune to our endeav-
ors as a community. Apart from the necessarily clannish declaration of "we
are this, and you are not," its deepest symbolism is inscribed in the sense of
brawny and visionary power that it communicates. And that is why claiming tribal membership can appear threatening to others.

My encounter with gay literature, with Warren, and Isherwood, and all
the others, was and remains a tribal ritual, a rite of passage into the larger
world of others like me, my brothers and my elders. In reading them, I discovered—or rather, reclaimed—parts of myself that the heterosexual
world refused to recognize as legitimately human. I became whole. In a
way, I grabbed my own salvation.

## EXCESS AND TRANSCENDENCE

If we accept Emile Durkheim's argument that religious feeling emerges
from what he calls "effervescent social environments," there can hardly be
any doubt that gay men have been religious more often than they perhaps
know or care to admit. Which gay man has not known, at some point in his

life, the very real feeling of ecstasy and union with others that comes from all-night dancing or the intense and prolonged search for sexual contact? These profoundly social activities awaken in us an equally profound sense of oneness and wholeness with others. Their effervescent quality, stimulated by alcohol, drugs, or adrenaline, gives rise to a feeling of *dépassement* or excess that literally takes us outside ourselves and binds us to the others. At this precise moment of social intensity, according to Durkheim, the sacred enters human consciousness.

As a sociologist, Durkheim was not prepared to admit a totally autonomous and independent existence to the sacred. His interest, a common one for intellectuals of his era, lay in uncovering the origins of religion, and he believed that he could find them in Australian aboriginal or totemic culture, since he thought that it contained the most primitive form of human religious expression then known. In his study, as we saw earlier, he argued that "excited" mental states, as expressed in ritual activity, give rise to an acute and dramatic sense of the overwhelming power of social bonds, and this sense of awe and wonder in the face of the omnipotence of these bonds stands behind the awesome emergence of the religious feeling. Religion, therefore, is another name for the power of society over the individual. The individual members of society, however, are not conscious of this. They react and respond to the fearful potency created by their own interactions. They name this mysterious power "the sacred."

Durkheim's theory opens up all sorts of interesting possibilities. Quite obviously, it allows for a far broader and more inclusive understanding of what constitutes religion and from whence it emerges. By extension, any intense social situation can be considered a potential source of religious feeling. "Religious feeling" here needs to be understood in the widest possible sense. It is not limited to formal institutional or liturgical expressions, or to a codified creed or set of theological tenets. Rather, it encompasses the full range of possibilities that are manifested in feelings of wholeness, oneness, transcendence, and ecstasy. The source of these feelings need not be identified with a particular divinity. It can be the result of a rich and complex social milieu or a series of especially engaging social interactions.

Many times I have stood alone in a crowded gay bar and felt an incredible sense of interconnection with the other gay men around me. This rather unique feeling emerges from a variety of sources. First, and most fundamentally, we all share a common identity and focus as gay men. Our lives, though very different from one another, intersect by virtue of the simple yet undeniable fact of our attraction to other men. Second, we are engaging in a ritual intrinsic to our culture as gay men, and we are doing so within the confines of one of our most important institutions, the gay bar. It is a safe and meaningful space for us. Third, an electricity and a sexual charge about our interactions bind us closely together. We may cruise, or we may not. We may look with desire, or we may choose to express our attraction more boldly. We may decide to go home with someone, or we may prefer to leave alone. The choices are ours, but they all stand within the realm of the possible. These unspoken possibilities solidify and cement our bonds. Finally, the energy created by our being together, often in close quarters under the influence of alcohol and pounding music, as exemplified by the particular dynamic of circuit parties, testifies to our visceral need for celebration and ecstatic excess in the midst of banality and blandness.

I believe that one of the truly spiritual qualities of gay men is the special capacity for celebration. I wish to suggest by this statement not that we are defined exclusively by our memorable parties, but that our place as marginal beings in society has sharpened our sensibilities to the compelling need for festivity and revelry as constituent parts of the human experience. Some may choose to argue that this is a negative function of marginality, that it reflects an inability to enter mainstream society and live fully as part of it, integrated into its institutions and cultural norms. My contention, however, is that marginality almost always implies excess because excess is such a powerful affirmation of humanity, a strategic quality needed to balance out the reasonableness of so much of what we do. Effervescence necessitates excess, and excess always demands transgression. It is not the ordinary and the lucid that need to be hemmed in by the knots of the sacred, but the taboo and the dirty, for therein resides what is most powerful.

It is unfashionable—if not downright immoral in the eyes of some—to extol the merits of excess in this day and age. Gay men have been accused, in different ways and at different times, of living excessively and outside the ethical boundaries that circumscribe "normal" human intercourse. Particularly now, at this critical juncture marked by the devastating legacy of AIDS, it seems irresponsible to reaffirm the necessity of leading a life of excess. If not irresponsible, then at least terribly incorrect politically. I believe, however, that one can live excessively and remain fully responsible for one's actions, and that to live spiritually is necessarily to function in an atmosphere of recalcitrance, as most true saints have demonstrated. "The underlying affinity between sanctity and transgression has never ceased to be felt. Even in the eyes of believers, the libertine is nearer to the saint than the man without desire," wrote Georges Bataille.[2] The transcendent and the sacred are found not in the orderly, but in the disorderly, the untidy, and the disheveled. The holy very often hovers about the perimeters of the most eccentrically erotic; it inhabits the land of desire.

The Greeks believed that rationality and irrationality were complementary aspects of human nature, and that one could not exist without the other. The spirit of rationality was embodied in Apollo, young god of beauty and light, while frenzy and folly were the domain of Dionysus, god of wine and sexual intemperance. The cult of Dionysus gave birth to theater. Apollo became a homoerotic icon celebrated in the arts, especially sculpture, and he transmuted into Hermes, the giver of arcane and secret knowledge.[3] Dionysus symbolized the ecstasy and abandonment associated with true religious feeling. In his celebrated novella *Death in Venice* (of which the film version by Luchino Visconti has become a gay classic) Thomas Mann, in symbolizing the nascent attraction of the writer Gustav Aschenbach for young Tadzio, recounts a dream of the main character in which every Dionysian excess is allowed free rein.[4] Aschenbach awakens exhausted and feverish, "hopelessly under the power of the demon,"[5] indifferent to what others may think of him. He knows he has crossed a line of no return, and he pursues Tadzio with the anguished devotion of bacchanals tracking their drunken god.

A story and a vision: a city in the early 1980s. The scene is a large mountaintop park in the middle of the night. Uncertain and a bit frightened, he grips the hand of his best friend who knows the way to that special corner where the worshipers gather nightly. The path is deathly quiet and pitch-black. He has heard horror stories about this place, ugly stories about gay bashings and police on horses running after men with pants around their ankles. The dark has always made him nervous, and he recalls the times, as a child, when he would run from the living room to his bedroom after having stayed up late to watch some scary old movie on television. The night air is cool and comfortable, the stirrings of early summer rustling the leaves of the maple trees. His friend silently pulls him off the path into some underbrush and forms suddenly appear in front of him. Male forms, all decked in denim and leather. His heart skips a bit, unsure whether desire or dread causes it. The moon is strangely luminous as it spatters silver threads on the ground. He really should not have drunk so much tonight. He would have gone home otherwise, safely ensconced in his own bed by now.

The sacred rite begins as the worshipers gather around the most beautiful of their number, the young god leaning seductively against a tree. Men in T-shirts with their jeans open, caressing themselves invitingly. He stares in awe and wonder, still unsure of why he is here. Groups form in circles and then disperse, naked shapes moving libidinously across the damp forest floor. Kneeling men raise their arms to naked chests, touching the chiseled bodies of the gods, eating the flesh and drinking the holy liquids. The dampness of the leaves mingles with the exciting mustiness and scent of males. Off in the distance, faintly, he hears the clatter of hooves. He fears these guardians of law and order, their heavy beasts bearing down sacrilegiously on this liturgy of desire and transgression. But he need not fear. It is only the mad god crossing the centuries, come to be with his own.

In the early hours of the morning, as he crawls quickly away from the shock of an impending sunrise, he knows that something important has happened to him, that he has finally come to know the ineffably transcendent.

## THAT SPECIAL GIFT

In gay circles, one often hears the old truism that lovers come and go, but friends last forever. Many gay men speak of friendship as the one truly spiritual aspect of their lives, referring to it in almost reverential terms. They remark on the comfort and joy it brings in good and bad times, and on the extraordinary grace it confers upon them. It is quite common for gay men to have one or more former lovers who have become close friends, and even to count exclusively sexual partners in their circle of friends. Young gay men growing up develop erotic attractions to other boys, often masking them as special friendships. While friendship certainly stands out as a universal experience, its shape is nonetheless strongly determined by the significant variables of gender and sexual preference. Friendship between straight men is undoubtedly not the same as friendship between gay men.

AIDS has been good for friendship, or rather friendship has been good to AIDS. It remains one of the rare and more precious boons of the epidemic. In *Love Undetectable*, Andrew Sullivan offers a moving meditation on the nature of friendship, its development throughout history, and its embodiment in the lives of gay men today. He begins his discussion with these eloquent words:

> I don't think I'm alone in thinking that the deepest legacy of the plague years is friendship. The duties demanded in a plague, it turned out, were the duties of friends: the kindness of near strangers, the support that asks the quietest of acknowledgments, the fear that can only be shared with someone stronger than a lover. In this sense, gay men were perhaps oddly well prepared for the trauma, socially primed more than many others to face the communal demands of plague. Denied a recognized family, often estranged from their natural one, they had learned in the few decades of their free existence that friendship was the nourishment that would enable them to survive and flourish. And having practiced such a virtue in good times, they were as astonished as everyone else to see how well they could deploy it in bad.[6]

Sullivan goes on to explore the understanding of friendship through the works of such thinkers, among others, as Augustine, Aristotle, Montaigne, Emerson, Freud, and Jesus. Conscious of the ascendancy of romantic love over friendship, calling love "the great modern enemy of friendship," he pleads passionately for a reassessment and a return of friendship as a virtue in human relationships, as something necessary and good to human existence. He suggests that gay men have been instrumental in sustaining it, but "only by default." He states: "Insofar as friendship was an incalculable strength of homosexuals during the calamity of AIDS, it merely showed, I think, how great a loss is our culture's general underestimation of this central human virtue."[7]

Gay men approach sexuality in its multiplicity of forms as just so many latent sites for experiencing wholeness and transcendence in their lives. Because sexuality is such a privileged venue for the expression of human physical intimacy, if not always emotional intensity, it is more potentiality than actuality. Gay friendships, on the other hand, seem to operate in the reverse. Either they are the result of a sublimated and therefore transformed erotic desire, or they are erotic desire fulfilled in the most inclusive and absolute way possible. That is why so many gay friendships begin as sexual encounters, and why they often last so long. The erotic dimension, vital to the sustenance of genuinely passionate human communication, is never totally absent. It acts as a current, keeping alive the promise of sexual communion. The holy is encountered in the pangs of desire, but it is equally experienced in the delicacy of friendship. We quite readily associate wholeness with sexual intimacy and exclusivity. As discussed earlier, however, this experience of union with others can also be a function of a collective identity and purpose. Perhaps more significantly, it further reveals itself in the delights and solace of friendship, in the special affinity that only two close friends can sustain together.

Like most people, I have had only a handful of intimate friends in my life, and many more acquaintances than I probably care to remember. In my youth, being somewhat withdrawn, I did not have many friends. The ones I did have, I clung to out of a sense of desperate possessiveness, as though they might evaporate overnight and I would be left standing alone against the big, bad world. In boarding school, friendship acquired an almost mystical power. You were very much defined by the people you hung around with, a typically adolescent take on life. The intensity of living together in a closed atmosphere, day in, day out, created a special energy and volatility that almost forced you to create strong bonds with others, very often upper classmates. When you became an upper classmate in turn, the adulation of the younger students was a formidable source of affirmation and respite.

Friendship is an acquired taste, just as it is a virtue that must be cultivated. In my time as a postulant and a novice, I discovered this basic fact of life. Maturity and experience certainly had something to do with it. Friendships were very intense in religious community. Forged in the give-and-take hothouse of communal life, they could blossom suddenly, or they required time and special circumstances to emerge from the ordinary and sometimes tedious fabric of the everyday. As might be expected, they were also deeply conditioned by the religious and spiritual atmosphere of the house. I recall, in particular, how three of us decided that we needed to deepen our experience of religious life by affirming the bonds of our friendship. Already quite close, we would sit in one another's rooms for hours at a time, bemoaning the fact that much of novitiate life was empty and sterile, not at all what we expected or wanted. We created our own ritual—or rather, we re-created one—in an effort to deepen our mutual dependence on one another, but also to strengthen our spiritual lives.

We gathered in the evening in one room. Sitting on the floor and holding hands, we prayed together, and we recounted the experience of our day. We shared a reading from Scripture. A chalice and a host were placed on the floor, and one of us recited the priestly words of consecration as the other two bowed their heads. We drank and ate the body and blood, embracing one another. It is strange, when you think about it, that we should have felt the need to copy the ritual of the Catholic mass in a setting that was already heavily imbibed with such ceremonies, almost as though we were unsure of the value and the validity of the real thing. We believed we were duplicating the intimacy and the conspiratorial intensity of the early Christians. When we were finished, we sometimes decided that we would "sleep over," and we would lie on the hardwood floor holding hands. There was never anything sexual about it. For us, there was a seamless fit between the eucharist we had just shared and this expression of our comradeship. It all was right; it made sense.

This search for a more intense form of community life also motivated an unusual experiment—unusual for that time and in that context—in which I engaged with another two of my novitiate companions in the latter part of our first year. Already close friends, we decided that we wanted to live together in community, but away from the formal novitiate context, while supporting ourselves and continuing our studies. The idea was to bridge the gap that we perceived between the church and the world, an ideal common to many young post–Vatican II seminarians of the early 1970s. Permission was granted by our religious superiors, and we embarked upon the great adventure for five or six months. We had committed ourselves to living within the norms of a communal religious life, attending mass together, praying as a group, and meeting on a regular basis with people we had chosen to "advise" us, a priest and a married couple with whom each of us had become close. I vividly remember the one time that we gathered in the evening with this couple to reflect on the similarities between our distinct "vocations" and commitments as married people and as priests-in-formation. The love and the warmth flowing between and among us, and the intensity of our exchange, remain engraved in my memory, even after all these partings and new beginnings.

The experiment, though interesting and formative, was not a success in the usual sense of the word. My two companions abandoned the seminary, while I returned only for another six months. Living this sort of arrangement was not easy, and it subtly transformed itself into a way of coping, for the first time in our lives, with the vagaries of autonomy and freedom. While it lasted, however, it captured my imagination and my enthusiasm, though I was always a bit disappointed by the somewhat more laid-back attitude of my two friends in terms of the self-discipline needed to maintain our religious household. We believed very much that we could cultivate intimacy, and that we could do this in the context and under the guise of a religious commitment. Here again, the two aspects of our lives were not mutually exclusive.

Naturally, one would occasionally fall in love, though one was not aware enough to be able to express it in these words. The border between friendship and love was not fixed, and I strongly suspect that we traversed it often in our minds, calling our transgression something else. Or at least, hoping that it was something else. Years later, when I was finally able to understand this period of my life from the vantage point of an out gay man, I came to the calm though unsurprising realization that the intensity of my seminary friendships was the expression of a sublimated erotic attraction, and that my need for community was a cry for meaning and sense in the midst of my confusion. This certainly does not mean that my friendships were not real or that my cry was not genuine. They stand, however, as signposts on the journey, as moments marking the twists and turns of my life.

Only one close friend remains from those special days. It has been close to thirty years, and he is still there in my life, providing a reassuring though physically distant presence. We have had, at times, a stormy relationship, but one that has gracefully and gratefully withstood the ravages of fate and the follies of human contingency. He is a passionate man, caring and committed, with a heart of gold that sometimes works against him. When I see him, as I must at least once a year, if I can, he renews my sagging spirits. We have a shared history and a shared belief in something bigger than either of us. He makes me crazy at times, as all sweet and dear friends must, but he makes me whole. I need him in my life, which would be considerably poorer if he were not a part of it. We have shared intimacy at every level, but the one that stays with us is the spiritual, for it grounds our friendship. Who would have thought that a boy from Canada would have met a kid from the American West one day at the door of the novitiate, and then written about him more than a quarter century later? Thank you, heavenly powers. In his book, Andrew Sullivan discusses the very moving passage in the *Confessions* in which Saint Augustine mourns the death of his friend. Augustine has the opportunity to reflect on life's transiency, to proclaim the "sweetness" of friendship and the ache that its absence brings. It is a testimonial full of pain and love. I know I will feel Augustine's anguish when my friend is finally taken from me. It is, I believe, the most fitting homage one can render to the enduring spiritual nature of true friendship.

## Intimacy and the Other

I am always amazed and gratified when I encounter a gay relationship that has lasted more than a year or two: amazed because it is not easy, even at the best of times, to live such a relationship in an open and honorable fashion, and gratified because it once again dispels the myth that gay men are promiscuous and therefore unable to sustain intimacy. When I stumble upon a gay couple who have been together for ten, twenty, thirty years, or more, I feel reverence. There is something incredibly beautiful and affirming about it because it is so rare. Such men, to me, are warriors and heroes of the tribe. They have made a contribution to gay liberation every bit as significant as that of the activists and politicos who have mounted the barricades in defense of our rights. Their contribution has been one of silent and persistent witness, proclaiming that love between men is very much within the realm of the possible, and then showing us how it can actually be lived out.

Though a stable gay relationship might appear ordinary and mainstream on the surface, the very fact of its existence makes it a transgressive act. After all, gay men are not supposed to be happy. Are they not creatures incapable of love, acting out some terrible sexual angst in deviant and destructive ways? They are narcissistic, and their relationships reflect a self-absorption that will ultimately leave them deserted and lonely. Moreover, they share the same gender. Where are the complementarity and wholeness that can come only from the merging of opposites? Do same-sex relations not go against the natural order of things, which sees the copulation of male and female as the source for new life and the propagation of the human species? These are all well-entrenched, though perhaps unspoken, stereotypes, still very much alive in our culture, and they are fed not so much by the laws of psychoanalysis as by the dogmas and creeds of established churches. They reflect the normative discourse of heterosexuality. When gay couples subvert this discourse by the simple but eloquent fact of their stability and happiness, they deal a rather extraordinary blow to its hegemony. They turn heterosexism on its head, exposing its unfounded claims as just so many socially constructed and culturally constrictive standards of behavior.

Apart from wonderful friends, I have been blessed with two significant gay relationships in my life. I lasted less than two years with my first lover, the one who really was instrumental in my coming out, but the intensity of the relationship and its subsequent breakup marked me for a long time. We were very different, and while I was deeply and selfishly in love, he would roam the byways of gay life, unbeknownst to me. I was extremely jealous and placed incredible pressure on the relationship by being so possessive. When he decided to live on his own, I was devastated. Though he eventually wanted to begin anew, I had by then met the man who would become the love of my life, the man with whom I have been now for more than twenty years.

I tend to be the type who needs stability. I have never been totally outside the confines of a primary relationship since leaving the seminary. I attribute this to a number of factors, some of which have to do with my childhood upbringing as well as the experience of cohabiting in close quarters with others from the beginning of my adolescence. Intimacy seems to come easily to me, once the barriers of reserve and control are overcome. I am conscious of this as a grace that is not given to all. Thus when my current companion entered my life some twenty-three years ago, the whole thing fell into place quite naturally, almost as though it were preordained. I suspect this is not an uncommon experience for many others who feel an equally powerful sense of having found the right person with whom to spend their lives. All of us expend our lives hankering after this gift, and some of us are fortunate enough to have it given to them.

What can I say about him, without slipping into the maudlin? He is sweet, and gentle, and terribly good for me. He has seen me through some rough spots, and we travel well together. He can be difficult, and stubborn, and terribly judgmental, just as I can at times. He has a soft heart, and his vulnerability brings tears to my eyes. He loves to read, and almost everything interests him. He is shy, and withdrawn, and awfully cute—well, to me at least. He is just fun to cuddle up to in bed. He says he loves me. A litany to my beloved. Scattered words meant to evoke what is intangible, what is perhaps reflected only in the eye of the beholder. A hymn to the wonder of companionship and love. And above all, a barrier against the absurdity and uncertainty of it all. An affirmation of gentle care and goodness in the face of sheer extinction.

Western culture emphasizes heterosexual monogamous love as the standard for the expression of the self. This emphasis is particularly striking when one considers the central importance given to marriage and the family, where the assumption is that they constitute the most complete path to happiness. Gays obviously do not fit into this banal paradigm, whether by design or by choice. Like most individuals, however, whatever their sexual proclivities, we crave companionship and the presence of that one special person. That person can be a lifelong partner, or he can be one stranger, among others, passing in the night. The difference, for us, is in the conflation of the erotic and the spiritual, and in the quality of their meeting.

In this chapter, I have put forward the idea that the gay experience of wholeness or integrity can be located along several vectors at once: in the gay "tribe," among friends, and in the committed relationship. I have equated wholeness with transcendence and with a sense of excess. I have gone one step further in suggesting that, as marginal individuals, we can claim spiritual wholeness only by moving beyond conformity to transgression, for only there can we find what we so desperately desire. As I will explore in the next chapter, religion and the erotic are closely allied. Adoration of the godhead and devotion to the fetishistic male body constitute flip sides of the same gold coin.

I share a rather extraordinary dream, or perhaps it is only a parable. I go home one night with a somewhat mysterious man I have met in a bar. There is nothing particularly frightening about this man, just something unusually appealing, as though he were driven by some special revelation. My new companion is sexy and attractive in a classically rugged way. We go to his house. Upon getting there, we have more drinks and a long and interesting conversation about many things, but mostly about Christian saints. I am puzzled, but assume that he has an academic, if somewhat unusual, interest in hagiography. Finally, we come to the business at hand. Being rather shy by nature, I am reluctant to undress in the living room, preferring the dark intimacy of a bedroom.

Upon entering his bedroom, I witness an incredible scene. There is a big double bed in the middle of the floor, and no other piece of furniture in the room. All around the floor, against the four walls, are life-sized statues of several dozen Catholic male saints: Francis of Assisi, Isaac Jogues, Roch, George, John the Evangelist, Paul, Francis Xavier, Peter, Ignatius of Loyola, Christopher, and John the Baptist, among others. In front of each burns a large votive lamp. I turn, only to see my companion appear in a loincloth with arrows protruding from his chest, arms, and legs. Saint Sebastian. I am immediately transported into a fit of ecstasy. We fall on the bed. I am merged with all the saints of my childhood, with all the intercessors of the divine godhead. The devotional life is really a life of obsession. It is a life of erotic play in the presence of the eternally true.

# 7

# Religion and Gay Culture

A LITANY AND A PRAYER:

Saint John the Baptist, cousin of the Redeemer, wild man of the
    desert, pray for us.
Saint John the Evangelist, beloved disciple and favorite companion
    of the Savior, seer of visions, pray for us.
Saint Paul of Tarsus, paragon of manly Christianity, whose teach-
    ing has scourged and oppressed us, pray for us. We forgive you.
Saint Sebastian, martyr and soldier, whose pierced naked body has
    been our solace and our delight, defender against pestilence,
    pray for us.
Saints Sergius and Bacchus, lovers and patrons of men in uniform,
    pray for us.[1]
Christopher, no longer saintly, whose muscular body carried the
    holy Child across stormy waters, pray for us.
Saint Francis, holy rebel and lover of nature, founder of communi-
    ties of poor men, whose body was scarred with the marks of the
    suffering Savior, pray for us.
All you holy popes, cardinals, and bishops, leaders of the church
    who have loved men in silence, pray for us. We expected more
    from you.

Saintly Christian Renatus, lover of Christ and adorer of Christ's
holy wounds, model of brotherhood, pray for us.

Saint Dominic Savio, youthful beauty and icon of purity, reliever
of our adolescent angst, pray for us.

Holy martyrs of Uganda, our black brothers, whose bodies were
consumed by fire rather than submit to abuse by authority, pray
for us.[2]

Oscar, poet and wit, victim of human intolerance and stupidity,
you who dared to speak our love and proclaim its beauty to the
world, pray for us.

Men of the death camps who wore the pink triangle, martyrs of
this gruesome and dark century, you who withstood the horror
of willful human evil, pray for us.

Harvey Milk, father of our liberation, pray for us.

All you men who suffered and died alone and neglected, victims of
the stigma of AIDS, pray for us.

All you men who have fallen prey to beatings and death because of
the irrational fear of sexual difference, pray for us.

Matthew Shepard, youthful martyr, pray for us.

Hear our prayer, O God. Grant that the intercession of these holy
men and martyrs will be for us a source of divine grace and
revelation. We pray that, through your goodness, they may
finally find comfort and rest in your holy arms. Send your
Spirit upon us, O God. May the shining example of these
saints inspire us to greater service and love for our brothers,
and may we never forget. Amen.

Yukio Mishima's *Confessions of a Mask* can lay claim to being one of the
most eloquent novels in world literature about gay coming of age. The
author writes about the time when his protagonist, aged twelve, first saw a
picture of Saint Sebastian in an art book:

I guessed it must be a depiction of a Christian martyrdom. But, as it
was painted by an esthetic painter of the eclectic school that derived
from the Renaissance, even this painting of the death of a Christian
saint has about it a strong flavor of paganism. The youth's body—it
might even be likened to that of Antinous, beloved of Hadrian,

whose beauty has been so often immortalized in sculpture—shows none of the traces of missionary hardship or decrepitude that are to be found in depictions of other saints; instead, there is only the springtime of youth, only light and beauty and pleasure.

His white and matchless nudity gleams against a background of dusk. His muscular arms, the arms of a praetorian guard accustomed to bending of bow and wielding of sword, are raised at a graceful angle, and his bound wrists are crossed directly over his head. His face is turned slightly upward and his eyes are open wide, gazing with profound tranquillity upon the glory of heaven. It is not pain that hovers about his straining chest, his tense abdomen, his slightly contorted hips, but some flicker of melancholy pleasure like music. Were it not for the arrows with their shafts deeply sunk into his left armpit and right side, he would seem more a Roman athlete resting from fatigue, leaning against a dusky tree in a garden.

The young boy reacts the only way he is able:

That day, the instant I looked upon the picture, my entire being trembled with some pagan joy. My blood soared up; my loins swelled as though in wrath. The monstrous part of me that was on the point of bursting awaited my use of it with unprecedented ardor, upbraiding me for my ignorance, panting indignantly. My hands, completely unconsciously, began a motion they had never been taught. I felt a secret, radiant something rise swift-footed to the attack from inside me. Suddenly it burst forth, bringing with it a blinding intoxication.[3]

This scene beautifully evokes the sexual awakening of a young boy. While the object of his adolescent desire has the voluptuous contours of the muscular male torso, the image unmistakably resembles that of a Christian saint, and he senses this immediately and keenly without really knowing. The object of sexual desire is a religious one, and one is left wondering how much this fact plays into the feverish intensity that inexplicably and quite suddenly grips him. To whom, or rather to what, is he responding? To the beautiful man or to the saint in ecstasy? To the religious icon or to the pornographic ideal? Is he having a sexual experience or a spiritual one? Does it really matter? These questions point to the thin line that separates *eros* from *religio*, the holy from the irrefutably and defiantly profane. As this text has argued, very often the two are manifestations of the same dynamic force.

A book by Richard Rambuss, entitled *Closet Devotions*,[4] states the case eloquently. A fine scholarly study of the prayer closet devotional style during the Renaissance, it also moves beyond the narrow historical data to suggest a recurring and intimate affinity between devotion and eroticism, particularly as this is expressed in same-sex desire. Looking at what he calls the "transgressive coordination of pleasure and devotion,"[5] Rambuss does not limit his analysis to a collection of English devotional verses, but looks to such sites as contemporary gay pornography and the work of AIDS-inspired artists to construct a theoretical venue for considering the interplay between religion and sex. Borrowing from the philosophical models of Georges Bataille and Michel Foucault, Rambuss argues that "the religious and the sexual are accorded adjacent psychic or, perhaps better, affective sites. It's in the mix of religion and the erotic—particularly . . . the erotically transgressive—that devotion becomes stimulated, heightened."[6] He states: "Religion . . . remains from a post-Enlightenment point of view a warehouse of perversions. Looking to religion has thus become a means of amplifying eroticism, of reinfusing it with an alluring transgressivity."[7]

Rambuss's argument opens up interesting possibilities. On a surface level, it makes contingent—and necessary—a sexual reading of religious symbols and rites. It calls for a radical reassessment of religious devotion in terms of a transgressive and nonnormative eroticism. The claim is made that devotional integrity is found at the various points of intersection of ecstatic religiosity and sexual deviance. In the Christian tradition, much of this devotion centers on the person of Christ, who is most assuredly male though also neutered in his full sexual expression as a man.[8] Rambuss demonstrates that the proliferation of same-sex devotional imagery, much of it far bolder and more explicit than we sometimes think, could be seen as an attempt to resexualize the Christ figure and to enter into intimate physical and spiritual contact with it. The prayer closet thus assumes a didactic and empowering role, "the technology by which the soul becomes a subject."[9] Through the intimacy of closet devotions, the borders between the holy and the profane are explored and ultimately trespassed, as they need to be if they are to retain any sort of viability. Just as Mishima's young boy masturbates alone one afternoon in front of the image of Saint Sebastian, thereby staking claim to his sexual persona, so the mystical verses of

Renaissance English devotional poets like John Donne and Richard Crashaw, kneeling alone in their prayer closets, point to a similar, though perhaps physically unexpressed, level of ejaculatory pleasure and devotion. Rambuss believes that this union of the erotic and the religious still operates, though it is increasingly seen as a dirty and scandalous thing:

> Erotic devotion—religion speaking of and as sex—does not suddenly disappear sometime in the seventeenth or the eighteenth century. But it does appear to be increasingly rezoned, with its all-exciting, unsettling flexions of amplified effect, to the closet. The prayer closet: a space where the body's "transports and motions" may speak, even heighten the devotion of the soul it houses. A space where the sacred may touch the transgressive, even the profane. A place where the naked, homoerotic clutch of Jacob and his God correlates to the lovemaking of husband and wife "behind the door." The prayer closet: a structure that still resides at the core of Christianity, though often now as a site of denial and scandal.[10]

The modern closet of the self-denying homosexual mirrors yet refutes the prayer closet of the English metaphysical poet. Site of possibility more than of affirmation, of rejection rather than worship, this closet continues to act as a closed space for the hidden transgression of normative erotic pleasure. It is same-sex pleasure denied, not asserted, though both closets operate in the realm of sublimation and substitution. The prayer closet is home to the sacred, the place the worshiper enters to encounter his god face-to-face and to express his desire for mystical and physical communion with his god. The gay closet is a locus of denial of the holy, because it is an emplacement for the imprisonment of the soul. The unopened gay closet has become "a site of denial and scandal," in a way far more nefarious and ugly than any prayer closet could ever be, even in its most religiously perverted form.

A contemporary gay thinker mentioned by Rambuss is the writer Michael Warner, whose essay "Tongues Untied: Memoirs of a Pentecostal Boyhood" he quotes. This essay is a classic of gay writing on religion. In it, Warner draws parallels between his upbringing in a Pentecostal household and his emergent identity as a gay man, thereby allowing him to reflect incisively and brilliantly on the meaning of each, and to extrapolate common themes between them. One of these themes is the way in which what he calls "ecstatic religion" and "the rhetorics of queer sexuality," by the very fact of their marginality, can and do construct alternate sites of meaning and worth.

> Religion makes available a language of ecstasy, a horizon of significance within which transgressions against the normal order of the world and the boundaries of self *can be seen as good things.* Pentecostalists don't get slain in the spirit just by rubbing themselves, or by redirecting some libido; they require a whole set of beliefs about the limitations of everyday calculations of self-interest, about the impoverishment of the world that does not willingly yield its increase to satisfy your lusts. In this way ecstatic religions can legitimate self-transgression, providing a meaningful framework for the sublime play of self-realization and self-dissolution.
> The bliss of Pentecostalism is, among other things, a radical downward revaluing of the world that despises Pentecostalists. Like all religions, Pentecostalism has a world-canceling moment; but its world-canceling gestures can also be a kind of social affirmation, in this case of a frequently despised minority. I suspect that the world-canceling rhetorics of queer sexuality work in a similar way. If you lick my nipple, the world suddenly seems comparatively insignificant. Ressentiment doubles your pleasure.[11]

In his discussion of Warner's essay, Rambuss refers to these forms of religious and sexual infractions as expressions of "ecstatically authorized transgression" and "salvific transgressivity," which "body forth divine operations that are world-altering."[12] Warner is saying that religion, particularly of the sort that encourages emotional expression, makes accessible a form of discourse and a space within which transgression and ecstasy—the pushing back of the boundaries of the everyday—are both possible and necessary, and moreover, good and positive. "World-canceling" is transformed, by a sublime twist of logic, into world-affirmation. The same, he argues, goes for gay erotic expression, which contains a similarly subversive streak. He takes an additional step, however. By using the word *ressentiment*, a French term denoting "spite" or "rancor," he hints at the direct correlation between marginality and pleasure, between being "cast out" and being able and willing to engage in forms of behavior that purposely subvert the norm and create the possibilities for genuine religious devotion and sexual pleasure. This *ressentiment* is not only something imposed from the outside; it acquires ontological status as a chosen state of mind. The formula sounds like a mantra: ostracism equals spite equals transgression equals ecstasy.

A similar mixture of emotive Christianity and sexual infraction is found in the work of controversial American performance artist Ron Athey.[13] Acknowledging his debt to a very strict religious background, which he claims to have rejected, Athey's pieces remain loaded with sophisticated religious symbolism and imagery, much of it referring to his fundamentalist Christian heritage. Using his own body as a canvas, Athey, who is HIV positive and a recovering addict, explores the ever shifting, unstable boundaries between sadomasochism and religious experience through the medium of body piercing. Such elements as blood, a powerful source of fear and contamination in the body of an HIV-positive person, are used to elicit reactions from people in an effort to unmask their irrational and deep-seated phobias.

I attended Athey's first-ever Canadian performance, entitled "The Solar Anus." It began with a video of the artist being tattooed on his backside. He then entered the room naked. All the while trancelike music was playing in the background. He knelt with his back to the audience, bending over to show us the real tattoo. In the background was a frozen film frame of his tattooed anus, rays of light emanating from it, and he bowed in front of it in a posture of adoration and respect. While bent over, he proceeded to withdraw, with the help of a hook, a long string of pearls from inside his body. He rose and donned fishnet stockings and high heels with huge black dildos affixed to them. Seated facing the audience, he placed a golden crown in the form of sun rays on his head. Sterilizing his face and the equipment he would use, he inserted hooks through his facial skin in six areas, stretching it and tying the hooks with string to the crown. His eyeballs turned back in their sockets, indicating that he was in a trance. The overall effect was eerie. He had the unmistakable look of a mask of Apollo, Greek god of the sun and of enlightenment. His legs in the air, he proceeded to sodomize himself with the dildos. The performance ended shortly thereafter with Athey bowing once again in adoration in front of the solar anus. It was, to say the least, a mesmerizing performance.

The tableau may seem extreme and pretentious at first, but on closer look, one sees that Athey is playing with the margins between religious symbolism and sexual excess. This performance uses as its central image one of the most socially ostracized parts of the human body—a part associated with dirt and pollution—and turns it into an object of veneration from which come beauty and pleasure. One is reminded of the passage in the Christian Scriptures where Jesus talks of "casting pearls before swine," though, in this case, the pearls emerge pristine white from what is perceived as a source of filth. The figure of Apollo presiding over the ceremony, the ultimate symbol of the god who is penetrated (or rather who penetrates himself), hearkens back to primitive androgynous rites of fertility. The subtext is unquestionably gay. Perhaps no other medium for sexual expression is as significant to gay culture as the anus. Athey shockingly reaffirms its preeminence as symbolic site of adoration and sexual exchange. Michael Warner's licked nipple pales by comparison, even though both acts are world-transcending in their subversion.

Whether it is the martyrdom of Saint Sebastian, Mishima's masturbating boy, the solitary pleasures of the prayer closet, or Warner's and Athey's Pentecostal fixations, such visions of sexual excess and religious ecstasy underscore one of the fundamental verities—if not *the* fundamental one—about religion and gay culture: that meaning arises through acts of infraction, whether they are sexual or religious. Heightened and transgressive sexuality can lead to ecstatic religiosity, and vice versa. Gay men, by virtue of their marginality, therefore have at their disposal a "natural" discursive universe for communing with the divine, if only they would tap into it.

## A GAY APPREHENSION OF THE HOLY

It is something of a platitude to claim that organized religion has not been good for gay men, just as it has not been good for other marginalized groups such as women and so-called heretics. There seems to be something strangely threatening to religious power when it enters into contact with individuals or collectivities who do not represent the sexual or the gender norm—or any other norm, for that matter. In some senses, this is a natural response by institutions that believe they have a right to exercise a monopoly and a control over moral codes, whether this right is claimed by virtue of "divine authority," "democratic privilege," or "reasons of state." Political power acts in similar ways, as does, though far more subtly, economic power. Gay men have therefore always had a suspicious view of religious institutions, as though these could turn at any instant and devour them. In many cases, the cynicism and distrust emerge from childhood or adolescent contexts where religion has played an oppressively stifling role.

This does not represent an unfounded fear, nor is it simply or only the realm of the paranoid expressing itself. It is, in many ways, a question of self-protection and a matter of self-respect. Why would anyone want to engage with, or be committed to, an institution whose historical record with respect to defending the integrity of his person and his rights is questionable at best? I suspect that most gay men who take religion seriously have queried this countless times. It is, without doubt, a legitimate and necessary question, one that allows us to retain some shred of human decency and pride.

Not long ago, I had an opportunity to confront this question. On the Sunday marking Montreal's gay pride celebrations, I attended morning mass in my local parish. A young, newly ordained priest was delivering the homily. Quite unexpectedly, he remarked that, on the preceding Saturday, he had met some young gay men and had had an interesting conversation with them about religion. *Very good,* I remember thinking, *it's important that people hear this.* Suddenly, however, the priest turned on us. He began pushing the church's party line and stated that, even though we must be accepted and loved, what we were—and what we did—was against natural law and therefore could not be endorsed or accepted. Angry and insulted, I walked out. I am a believing and sometimes practicing Catholic. I love the church and all it represents. But how could I just sit there and accept this denigration of my very person from the mouth of one of the church's representatives? How can we sustain our love for this institution, yet still hold it accountable? Therein lies the dilemma. Therein also lies the promise of a resolution, for only in loving completely can we hope to correct.

Perhaps, as many continue to claim, religion and gay culture do not belong together. Perhaps they are mutually exclusive spheres, and the best we can hope for is a fragile stalemate, a draw at high noon. Yes, perhaps indeed. The pitfalls of religious institutions with respect to homosexuality are legion, and gay men are right to be wary of them. Yet gay men keep believing. We continue to attend church and temple, to pray and to meditate, to come together to celebrate and to worship. What explains this almost irrational need to remain part of what is certainly a homophobic— and somewhat passé, in the eyes of some—cultural institution? What is

this "pull" that the religious exerts on us as gay men? Even more fundamentally, do we have a particularly unique way of apprehending the holy,
of understanding the contours and the exigencies of its highly fortuitous,
though powerful, existence? What makes us, as gay men, specifically religious, if at all? Is there something about gay culture that opens us to a
sense of the sacred? Important questions all, though they sometimes
reflect our nascent insecurities more than our certainties.

I have argued that our religiosity is marked by our marginality, and that
it is mainly transgressive in character. I should like to suggest two further
elements: receptivity and perversity, or an attitude of openness and one of
rebellion. In some ways, these could be seen as opposite ends of the spectrum, though they constitute mutually necessary and dependent cofactors
in our spiritual development. Receptivity and perversity reflect what we
*are or should be* in society, as well as how we choose to constitute ourselves
as persons. These are sociological and existential categories, one emerging
from our social position, the other, from our erotic calling and the choices
flowing from it. We are rebellious because we are marginal, and we are
receptive because that is how we love.

In the days before the advent of gay liberation, none of us really wanted
to be known as a homosexual. We had "a history of shadows," as a novel
recounting that time so aptly puts it.[14] We were a hidden, discrete race,
cautious in our dealings and subtle in the signals we emitted in recognizing
one another. To be known as a homosexual implied danger and risk—to
ourselves, our jobs, our parents, our wives and children. The most vivid
and destructive example of what might happen to us was embodied in the
famous McCarthy witch-hunts of the 1950s, which destroyed both lives
and careers. Interestingly enough, we were "thrown in" with that other
great subversive of the American way of life, the ungodly Communist. We
were supposedly seen as a threat to national security because we could be
blackmailed. I suspect the real reason had much more to do with the moral
threat we were thought to pose to American manhood, to say nothing of
the self-hating homophobia of key investigators such as Roy Cohn.[15] As
enamored as the United States may have been with the cocky androgyny of
a James Dean, it could not afford to let the queers run rampant.

With the winds of the 1960s came the militancy of gay liberation and
its shattering of traditional canons of thought and action. Suddenly, a
whole new level of experience and affirmation was open to us, one that
made it possible yet necessary for us to emerge from the shadows. The

sweet excesses of the 1970s followed upon this time of liberation, excesses fueled by years of sublimation and the compelling need to create spaces for ourselves in which to play and live. We made sexuality a way of life, a defiant statement of difference and pride. It was a heady and passionate time, an era of savage masculinity and limitless sexual experimentation. It was also a necessary time.

The 1980s came on boldly and confidently, compelling us, despite our optimism, to confront the harsh boundaries of biological survival of the fittest, as our sculpted bodies became a battlefield on which was dependent the livelihood of a virus. Overnight, we learned to negotiate with death and the grief and vermin tearing at our insides. We transformed ourselves into an angry tribe, striking out blindly at those who would kill us through benign or maliciously stupid neglect. We rose to the occasion, and in the process we fundamentally altered who we were and how we loved.

We have been a rebellious bunch—and not only in this generation, but down through history. We continue to be a perverse agent in society and culture, edging them toward transformation and change. Because we are seen and defined by "the other" as perverts, we act perversely—"different from what is reasonable or required," as the *Oxford Dictionary* puts it. It can be revealing to look at synonyms for "perverse," words such as "contrary," "insubordinate," "naughty," "obstinate," and "head-strong," all of them positive and necessary to the ongoing development of an open and dynamic society. We need to equate perversion and rebellion with prophecy, a religious word if ever there was one. What are prophecy and prophets, if not religious agents of change?

The religious impulse is a strangely ambivalent one. It can perform two almost opposing cultural roles: as a strong force for stability and cohesion, or as a powerful and dynamic impetus for change. Most religions are born as movements that stand in an almost diametrical opposition to the society in which they find themselves. Most emerge as sects (consider the origins of Christianity) and then move on to become institutions in their own right. This process, though modulated by time and historical circumstance, is unavoidable. Sects become churches, which become, in turn, venues of social control and normative discourse. Both Karl Marx and Max Weber, in contradistinction to Emile Durkheim, saw a critical role for religion in society, one in which it could play—and has played—the role of "change agent."[16] Religion deals in the realms of ideals and possibilities, of truth and universal good, of divine plans and what cannot be fully attainable in the here and now. Though Marx foresaw the need eventually to surpass religion in a classless society, he recognized its necessary social function when he referred to it as "the heart of a heartless world" and "the sigh of the oppressed creature." Even today, many have been the social revolutions that have claimed a Marxist and a Christian inspiration. Equally important, Weber's elaboration of and application of such terms as "ideal types" and "charisma," most notably with respect to his work on the economy and religion, delineate a profile of religion as source of social and cultural transformation.

Religion, as with gay culture, essentially acts as a culturally prophetic medium. It is, in sum, utopian. It holds out a model for what is possible (whether brotherhood, love, or even nirvana), but is not really attainable given the transience and contingency of "the here below" and the foibles of humankind. Too often, this socially marginal positioning of religion is neglected at the expense of its far more traditional and comfortable role as source of institutional stability and cultural validation. Yet if the holy brings chaos and uncertainty in its stead—if it is socially disruptive and therefore prophetic—then it is indeed perverse and marginal. The holy is never quite mainstream. Gay culture is, I believe, fundamentally the same: never quite normal or accepted, always showing that there are different and unusual ways of loving and being, calling society to a critically engaged stance in terms of its own self-definition. Gay men are prophets, I would affirm, much as religious virtuosi have been and still are.

Gay men exist in the world as sexual beings. While this is undoubtedly true for all persons, it is particularly so for homosexuals. It is so because that is how we are defined and pegged by the norm, and also because that is how we choose to relate to the norm. For the gay man—as for the black man, the native person, the woman, or the member of an ethnic group— how one exists in the world is conditioned by one's identity, heritage, and quality of experience as someone outside the mean. As men who are attracted sexually and emotionally to other men, we stand outside the mean. We cannot be socially controlled as other males are because, for us, every other male is a potential source of sexual adventure, and therefore a signifier of deviance and aberration in terms of what the heterosexual standard tells us males are really meant for. Even—or rather, especially—in our sexual acts, we transgress.

A prerequisite of a genuinely spiritual life is the ability to be open to the sacred, to let oneself be invested with, and surrounded by, its all-pervasive presence. Spirituality implies a relationship, and it necessitates a commitment. Without this ability to enter into an intimate communion with the source of our inspiration and worship, spirituality becomes little more than the circular search for a quick feel-good fix. One must be receptive to the holy, open to its call, and porous to its influence. The proper attitude for the believer is that of an expectant passivity, the "waiting upon God" so often alluded to by the great Christian mystics. One places oneself in a position of alert supplication, waiting to be summoned forth and filled, not with earthly power, but with the light of divine grace and benediction. For many, and particularly for men generally, this is not an easy or a comfortable state to be in. We want quick contact, and we want it now. We want to be the ones in charge, the aggressive ones.

Gay men threaten the sexuality of straight men (and sometimes of straight women, though for different reasons) because their experience of sexuality and of the dynamics of sex roles includes the taboo of receptive intercourse. Insecure heterosexual men can perceive this as a threat to their sexual hegemony, blurring gender roles and hinting at the possibility that all men can potentially desire and enjoy the same experience. This openness to a willful condition of receptivity in the sexual act is, I would argue, one of the distinguishing marks of gay male sexuality, something not always readily understood and accepted in a heterosexist, patriarchal culture. It also goes beyond the isolated sex act or our concomitant erotic choices. Our sense of self, and of our place in the world, I would suggest, is intimately tied up with our openness to passivity and to active receptivity. This represents a fundamentally spiritual attitude toward life.

There is a sense in which, for the Christian at least, the central icon of the half-naked Christ suffering and dying on the cross touches on some deep-seated physical urge bordering on the erotic. In this image, the holy is the very embodiment of all that is most passive and receptive, "the lamb brought to slaughter," the plaything of political and religious power. The theological meaning attached to this portrait of vulnerability implies that redemption is truly effected through such apparent weakness and impotence. Passivity is transformed, and it becomes the means by which identity and power are actively engaged. The attractive figure of Christ on the cross—the perfect illustration of physical receptivity—assumes an exemplary role for gay men because its language of vulnerability is really the language of spiritual potency.

This discourse of insertion and receptivity, whether reflected in the erotically charged verses of the prayer closet devotees or the equally carnal theological statements of the Harmonist Brotherhood, points to a uniquely gay male way of understanding and appropriating the holy. In this sense, the holy, for gay men, is assuredly and defiantly male, the embodiment of creative masculine energy and authority. It is a holy that arrives to seize and penetrate the believer, and fill him with inspiration and gratitude. Our eroticism delineates the contours of our faith, in the same way that it colors the texture and the shape of all other segments of our lives.

## THE "PROBLEM" OF GAY SPIRITUALITY

Is gay spirituality really problematic? And if it is, why? In concluding this book, I would like to reflect briefly on some of the larger issues that have emerged thus far. I return to an observation made in chapter 1, where I asked whether gay spirituality was a genuine form of religiosity, or whether it was only another example, though perhaps a more sophisticated one, of gay identity politics. I admit that I ducked my own question. I retreated into the "objective" stance of the sociologist of religion, observing that all manner of religious life "is worthy of respect and investigation." I did attempt a preliminary response, however. I indicated that the question was a serious one, and that I believed gay spirituality to be two things at once—a manifestation of genuine religious belief *and* a type of identity politics. The two, I stated confidently, "are not mutually exclusive." I hope these pages have demonstrated the relative truth of this observation.

Queer theorists and activists may well choose to disagree with me, and I am sympathetic to their challenge. They will remind me of the insidious and oppressive nature of religion, always and everywhere, and I may nod in agreement. They will return to that old standby, Marxism, and talk of religion as a form of "false consciousness," as something that detracts from the urgency of unmasking and challenging the sites of abusive power in contemporary culture. Again, I am not necessarily at variance with these views. As a matter of course, I believe one should be wary not only of religion, but of all other forms of institutional power in society that have the very real potential of sinking into absolutism. The queer critique of religion rings particularly true because religion has been the most abusive of all institutions toward homosexuality in general, and gay and lesbian persons in particular, in the West. This legacy is not so easily dismissed, try as we may to couch it in the amorphous and relatively harmless language of spirituality.

Some will say that gay spirituality is about liberation, and here again one stumbles upon a grain of truth. Reappropriation is a necessary yet painful part of liberation. As was discussed in several passages in this book, attempts by gay men to reclaim and recontextualize religion are essential. They constitute part of the affirmative process we engage in when staking out our place in the world. Through these efforts, we validate our religious experience, and we ultimately legitimize ourselves and our community. In the wonderful Cuban film *Strawberry and Chocolate*,[17] the main character, who is gay, has created for himself a world where, despite the oppressive politics of his country, he very intelligently reappropriates the literary, musical, and religious artifacts that mark and reveal his difference, thereby revaluing his experience as a homosexual. Naturally, this is all very subversive, and he will be brought in by the authorities, but not before he has awakened the spirit of defiance and planted questions of sexual uncertainty in the mind of another young Cuban. In reclaiming our place, we also deconstruct and subvert what is unquestionably or naively taken for granted.

The problem of gay spirituality—if there can be said to be one—is part and parcel of the problem of gay identity politics generally. Only in the context of this larger issue can the contingency of gay spirituality be properly situated and understood. In referring to "the problem" of gay identity politics, I raise the oft-debated question of how far we should go, in either direction, in *integrating ourselves with* or in *differentiating ourselves from* the heterosexually normative. Is it both sufficient and necessary to claim a separate identity, and is this a solid enough base upon which to create a community and demand equality with others? Or is there another political strategy, one that will move beyond identity to a place of permanent normative transgression? Should the gay identity be so fixed and exclusive, as many queers ask, or should it be part of an ever-moving panoply of positions and performance options? Strategically speaking, is queer identity the best form of politics? These questions can have a familiar echo when applied to gay spirituality. As much as we interrogate our politics, we should also scrutinize and query our spirituality. Do we really need our own forms of religiosity, in sum, and are they the best means to advance our cause socially, politically, and culturally? One might even add, not without cringing, "and economically"?

I will admit that there is a dual danger inherent to gay spirituality. The first is that it will distract us from politics; the second is that it will become politics. Actually, this is no different from the challenges (temptations, perhaps?) faced by most, if not all, religious movements and institutions: How to be "in this world," while not being quite "of it"? If one accepts that religion is a legitimate and necessary part of the human experience, then whether it is gay is secondary, indeed almost irrelevant. But no form of spirituality should become an iron-clad refuge from the world, sheltering us from its moral imperatives and the very real and necessary task of transforming it. This is particularly the case for the manifestations of religious conviction and belief, such as gay spirituality, that are the expression of the dynamics of social exclusion. Otherwise, such spiritualities betray their calling and, ultimately, their adherents.

Equally important, gay spirituality should not, and cannot, be transformed exclusively into a political act, though it is this by virtue of its role as the expression of cultural marginality. To evacuate any of its religious—and therefore transcendent—content or meaning is equally destructive of its ultimate value and worth. Gay spirituality exists primarily as a form of religious expression, and we must acknowledge and respect this. I have advocated for a reading of the contemporary gay experience as religious experience. In doing so, I am aware that one must exercise caution, otherwise all is thrown together rather haphazardly and meaninglessly. This reading sees the work of divine grace in the lives of gay men, both collectively and individually. While I may be accused more of theologizing than of doing sociology, I will retort that good sociology is good theology, particularly when it comes to understanding the dimensions of the sacred.

Is there a future for gay spirituality? The question is more than rhetorical. As long as there are gay men trying to make sense of their position of marginality in this world, there will be some form of gay spiritual expression, for it is a compelling necessity imposed on us by force and by circumstance. I suggested in an earlier chapter that gay writers have generally approached the problem of the sacred in gay lives in one of four broad ways: by providing counterinterpretations of commonly accepted theological or historical facts (the apologetic mode), by offering paradigms of positive psychospiritual health (the therapeutic mode), by suggesting ethical parameters for gay men's relations with the world and with one another (the ecological mode), and by reflecting critically on the individual religious upbringing and experience of gay men (the autobiographical mode). On a considerably smaller scale, each one of us, in the depths of his own soul, engages in these four "spiritual exercises," for each one of us must struggle with what it means to be gay at this time and in this place. When you think about it, each one of us is really *all* of us.

What is exciting and not at all problematic about gay spirituality is that the outcast, the pervert, has finally entered the holy of holies and has dared to call his god "queer." And of that, we can all be justifiably proud and grateful. It calls for a celebration.

# Afterword

## "Canadian, Québécois, Catholic . . . and Queer"

THROUGHOUT THE WRITING of this book, I have struggled with a variety of identities. At every turn, I have had to position myself with respect to my nationality, my religion, my sexual preference, and ultimately, my intellectual integrity. This book represents many things. It is, first and foremost I hope, a book of observation and reflection. I have tried to step back and take a critical look at what it means to be gay today, and what this might imply for an authentically spiritual way of existing in the world. The book is also self-revelatory, even though I was hesitant initially to write it in this way. My original intent was to limit myself to a sociological study of gay spirituality, something that could be used in classes and seminars, and would ultimately be "safer" for me, as it might be for any gay author. At the suggestion of my editor, however, I decided to bring in a much more personal dimension. I did this for two reasons: because it is far more interesting for the reader, and because it allows me to tap into my experience as a way of bringing my observations to life. In this sense, the book has been good for me. It has allowed me to look back and, in so doing, to enrich moments and people in my life by placing them in a meaningful perspective. I am most grateful for this rare opportunity. Finally, the book has been a declaration of love and faith: of love and solidarity for my gay brothers, and of faith in my religious heritage that is so much a part of who I am, and that I sometimes acutely feel I neglect at my emotional peril.

I have vacillated between and among identities throughout my life. American-born of French Canadian parents, I grew up speaking French at home and English in school. I have lived in the United States and in French- and English-speaking Canada. I have been a devout Roman Catholic—going so far as to want to enter the priesthood—and a considerably less pious scholar and dissector of religion. I still attend church when I feel the urge, and it seems to be growing stronger with each passing year. I am intensely conscious of, and grateful for, my French heritage, and my politics are not unsympathetic to the sovereign aspirations of Quebec, though I function in a largely English-speaking environment on a daily basis. I have had sex with both men and women, and I considered myself bisexual for a long time. I am a gay man pushing fifty who appreciates the antics and wild challenges of queer boys and girls, and who functions, as we all must do, in a straight world. And now here I am, a new Canadian author with a U.S. publisher, writing about a topic that is, in many ways, a quintessentially U.S. one. To say the least, mine has been, and continues to be, an interesting voyage.

Increasingly, the modern condition is one comprising synchronous identities. In this sense, my story could be considered exemplary. I am an amalgam of simultaneously existing persons: bilingual, bicultural, and even sometimes bisexual. If I could think of a word denoting belief in two religious ideals coexisting at once, I would use it, though I am not quite sure what that might be or even what it might mean—perhaps "ecumenical" would come close. We all operate in more than one world at once, and we all adopt different and sometimes competing roles at particular points in our lives. For some, it is a question of survival; for others, it is a matter of deliberate and strategic choice. But there is a critical difference between these masks we all wear and the roles we choose or are forced to perform, and an existential state of polymorphism. The former are social and cultural exigencies; the latter is a way of being. The former states imply and facilitate integration; the latter necessitates and reinforces difference and marginality. It is not a bad condition to be in, actually. It does mean, however, that one is never quite sure where one best belongs.

My sexual and religious identities have stood side by side, each feeding off and conditioning the other, though not always to their mutual benefit. Younger, I had a sadly exaggerated sense of guilt with respect to sexual matters, particularly when I was in the seminary, to the point that I developed an unhealthy obsession with masturbation as a sin. Though compulsive masturbation is common for young boys, the staunch Roman Catholicism in which I was raised inculcated me with a misplaced sense that it was very wrong—another example of the Christian obsession with the human body as source of pollution and evil. On the other hand, the rich trappings of my pre–Vatican II faith, I believe, have taught me much about the liturgical and ritualistic aspects of apparently simple human behavior. Such a double standard may well be unavoidable. Perhaps it helps to explain why only someone like me can speak of gay sex and the sacred in the same breath, why I can be both queer and Catholic. It is a comfortably hazy identity for me, a way of ennobling my guilt and my sin, which, when you think about it, is really what religion has always done.

Contemporary individuals are both voyeurs and exhibitionists because we inhabit a vicarious media culture of fleeting and transitory pleasures. We all believe sincerely that our experience is unique, and to a large extent it is. To make sense of it at times, we feel we need to display it for the world to see and gawk at. Our culture is also talkative. We stand ever eager to share with others our innermost secrets and insights, confident that they hold the power to re-create us as more effectively human persons. I approached the writing of this book with mixed feelings. If the book was to speak with any measure of validity to the religious experience of gay men, I needed to be honest about myself, thereby opening my person to a measure of scrutiny. I was also aware that I was playing the game of the talkative culture, providing others with a vicarious peep into my life, thoughts, and fantasies, sexual or otherwise. I asked myself whether, in doing so, I was cheapening my experience.

The question appears unavoidable in a book like this, which rests on an analysis of spiritual and sexual identities, and which must struggle with elements drawn from one's life. I am conscious that this is a therapeutic piece of work, as I would think any kind of memoir writing is, though these pages do not aspire to such heights. I prefer to think of my effort as a meditation, which may explain the eclectic mixture of styles: at times, partly cultural and social analysis; at others, theological reflection. The therapy was essential at this point in my life, for this book marks a fork in the road, a shifting of priorities and perspectives for me. From closeted, I have moved to a radical appreciation of my uniqueness as a gay man. From religiously neutral, I have traveled to a space and a time that summon me to spiritual engagement. And yes, from a position of assimilation, I have shifted to one of queer separation. We are our politics, almost as much as we are the sum of our experience.

Because I am a child of the boomer generation and of Stonewall, identity is undoubtedly more important to me than it is to my younger queer brothers and sisters, in large part because it was all we had to affirm our difference and all we needed to live it out. My final words are therefore ones of conciliation and of hope, but also of warning. The conciliation and the hope emerge from a belief in the absolute necessity of dialogue and care for one another, regardless of generational alliances. If we refuse, we are doomed, for the majority will not be vigilant on our behalf. We need to respect our gay ancestors, those whose courage has made our pride almost trendy. The warning is a spiritual one. Let us never lose respect for the sacredness of our passion and the beauty of our calling, for then we will have truly sinned against nature.

# Notes

## Preface

1. Ronald E. Long, "The Sacrality of Male Beauty and Homosex: A Neglected Factor in the Understanding of Contemporary Gay Reality," in *Que(e)rying Religion: A Critical Anthology*, ed. Gary David Comstock and Susan E. Henking (New York: Continuum, 1997), 273. This essay is one of the more incisive in the analysis of gay spirituality. Its theoretical possibilities have yet to be fully explored.

## 1. A Window on Gay Identity

1. See Brian Bouldrey, ed., *Wrestling with the Angel: Faith and Religion in the Lives of Gay Men* (New York: Riverhead Books, 1995).

2. For an overview and analysis of some gay men's ways of being religious, from the perspective of individual experience, see ibid.; Richard P. Hardy, *Loving Men: Gay Partners, Spirituality, and AIDS* (New York: Continuum, 1998); David Shallenberger, *Reclaiming the Spirit: Gay Men and Lesbians Come to Terms with Religion* (New Brunswick, N.J.: Rutgers University Press, 1998); and Peter Sweasey, *From Queer to Eternity: Spirituality in the Lives of Lesbians, Gay & Bisexual People* (London: Cassell, 1997).

3. See Annamarie Jagose, *Queer Theory: An Introduction* (New York: New York University Press, 1996). For the neophyte, this book, as its title indicates, provides an excellent theoretical and historical introduction to the complexities of queer theory. See also Michael Warner, ed., *Fear of a Queer Planet: Queer Politics and Social Theory* (Minneapolis: University of Minnesota Press, 1993).

4. See Emile Durkheim's classic study in the sociology of religion, *The Elementary Forms of the Religious Life* (New York: Free Press, 1915).

5. Feminist or womyn's spirituality has produced innumerable works. Among the more important, see Mary Daly, *Beyond God the Father: Toward a Philosophy of Women's Liberation* (Boston: Beacon Press, 1985) and *The Church and the Second Sex* (Boston: Beacon Press, 1985); Carol Ochs, *Behind the Sex of God* (Boston: Beacon Press, 1977); and Rosemary Radford Ruether, *Women-Church: Theology and Practice* (San Francisco: Harper & Row, 1985). For a discussion and analysis of women's rituals, see the recent study by Lesley A. Northup, *Ritualizing Women* (Cleveland: The Pilgrim Press, 1997).

## 2. Understanding Gay Spirituality

1. The cartoon was by Mike Luckovich, and it appeared in the *Atlanta Constitution*; its date is unknown.

2. See Denise Carmody and John Carmody, "Homosexuality and Roman Catholicism," in *Homosexuality and World Religions*, ed. Arlene Swidler (Valley Forge, Pa.: Trinity Press International, 1993), 135–48.

3. The pink triangle was the identifying mark that homosexuals had to wear in Nazi concentration camps. It has become one of the major symbols of gay and lesbian pride worldwide. The pink triangle was the lowest "grade" in the camp hierarchy of prisoners. Homosexuals are almost never remembered when it comes to commemorations of the victims of Nazism, to say nothing of the Holocaust. As a group of victims, they have never been financially compensated. In the minds of many persons, they were and remain criminals rather than innocent victims. This fact only goes to show how ingrained homophobia really is, even when it comes to human suffering.

4. By far, the most influential text in the theology of liberation is Gustavo Gutiérrez's *A Theology of Liberation* (Maryknoll, N.Y.: Orbis Books, 1973). See also Leonardo Boff and Clodovis Boff, *Introducing Liberation Theology* (Maryknoll, N.Y.: Orbis Books, 1987). For a slightly more general expression of this form of theology in a North American context, see Gregory Baum, *Compassion and Solidarity: The Church for Others* (Toronto: CBC Enterprises, 1987) and "The Homosexual Condition and Political Responsibility," in *A Challenge to Love: Gays and Lesbians in the Church*, ed. Robert Nugent (New York: Crossroad, 1983), 38–51.

5. "The Sisters of Perpetual Indulgence, an order of 'genderfuck' drag nuns based in San Francisco, invoke the power of female deities in rituals meant to support and protect gay people and others. In their rites, as in those of the Radical Faeries, the Goddess is sometimes invoked in a 'camp' or carnivalesque form" (Randy P. Conner, *Blossom of Bone: Reclaiming the Connections between Homoeroticism and the Sacred* [San Francisco: HarperSanFrancisco, 1993], 268). The Sisters represent a rather unique manifestation of gay spirituality. They

most certainly are a spoof on religion, urging gay men, "Give up the guilt!" Yet they perform an interesting ritual role by virtue of the fact that they very often serve as "exorcists," expelling "bad spirits" from gay celebrations. The fact that the Sisters are bearded men dressed in nuns' habits, and therefore a manifestation of drag culture, makes their interventions satirical in the extreme.

6. This theoretical understanding of Christian spirituality was elaborated in the context of a lecture on the staunchly Roman Catholic Opus Dei movement, which I attended at the Université de Montréal in 1999.

7. *Mother Jones*, November/December 1997.

8. Nancy Wilson, "Fear of Faith," *Harvard Gay & Lesbian Review* 3, no. 4 (fall 1996): 18.

9. William Clossen James, *Locations of the Sacred: Essays on Religion, Literature, and Canadian Culture* (Waterloo, Ont.: Wilfrid Laurier University Press, 1998), 5.

10. For an excellent analysis of the New Age "movement," see Wouter J. Hanegraaff, *New Age Religion and Western Culture: Esotericism in the Mirror of Secular Thought* (Leiden: E. J. Brill, 1996).

11. I refer here to the incredible appeal of such manifestations of popular culture as the television series *The X Files*, which plays upon the contemporary fascination with conspiracy theories and alternative forms of spiritual and paranormal insight, in particular those related most directly to the existence and presence on earth of extraterrestrials.

12. Gay literature has really come into its own since the late 1970s and early 1980s. It has produced a rich corpus of works, which would be too lengthy to enumerate here. For some of the earlier books, see, among many others, Robert Ferro, *The Family of Max Desir* (New York: New American Library, 1983); Andrew Holleran, *Dancer from the Dance* (New York: William Morrow, 1978); Larry Kramer, *Faggots* (New York: Warner, 1978); David Leavitt, *Family Dancing* (New York: Warner, 1983); and Edmund White, *A Boy's Own Story* (New York: New American Library, 1982) and *The Beautiful Room Is Empty* (New York: Random House, 1988). There is also an extensive and rather interesting subgenre known as AIDS literature. See, in this regard, Timothy F. Murphy and Suzanne Poirier, eds., *Writing AIDS: Gay Literature, Language, and Analysis* (New York: Columbia University Press, 1993); and the remarkable collection of stories by Edmund White and Adam Mars-Jones, *The Darker Proof: Stories from a Crisis* (New York: New American Library, 1988).

13. The corporal (because they refer to the body) works of mercy are as follows: to feed the hungry, to give drink to the thirsty, to shelter the homeless, to clothe the naked, to visit the imprisoned, to nurture the sick, and to comfort the dying.

14. As will be explained later in this chapter, I use Stonewall as a convenient symbolic marker because it is a culturally significant event for the gay

community. See the important collection of gay liberation writings, Karla Jay and Allen Young, eds., *Out of the Closets: Voices of Gay Liberation* (New York: Pyramid Books, 1974).

15. See Carmody and Carmody, "Homosexuality and Roman Catholicism." The best expression of this teaching is Pope Paul VI's controversial 1968 encyclical *Humanae Vitae* (On Human Life).

16. The most influential thinker by far is Michel Foucault. See, in French, his *Histoire de la sexualité 1: la volonté de savoir* (Paris: Editions Gallimard, 1976). See also Bob Gallagher and Alexander Wilson, "Sex and the Politics of Identity: An Interview with Michel Foucault," in *Gay Spirit: Myth and Meaning*, ed. Mark Thompson (New York: St. Martin's Press, 1987), 25–35; and David Halperin's comprehensive study of Foucault's theoretical framework, *Saint Foucault: Towards a Gay Hagiography* (New York: Oxford University Press, 1995).

17. See, among others, George Chauncey Jr., *Gay New York: Gender, Urban Culture, and the Making of the Gay Male World, 1890–1940* (New York: Basic Books, 1994); John D'Emilio, *Sexual Politics, Sexual Communities: The Making of a Homosexual Minority in the United States 1940–1970* (Chicago: University of Chicago Press, 1983); David Greenberg, *The Construction of Homosexuality* (Chicago: University of Chicago Press, 1988); David Halperin, *One Hundred Years of Homosexuality and Other Essays on Greek Love* (New York: Routledge, 1990); Gilbert Herdt, *Same Sex, Different Cultures: Exploring Gay and Lesbian Lives* (Boulder: Westview Press, 1997); and Jeffrey Weeks, *Coming Out: Homosexual Politics in Britain from the Nineteenth Century to the Present* (London: Quartet Books, 1977).

18. The Stonewall Inn was a Mafia-controlled, rather seedy transvestite and hustler bar in Greenwich Village in New York City. The Stonewall riots took place on the weekend of June 27, 1969.

19. Jagose, *Queer Theory*, 30.

20. On Edward Carpenter, see Edward Carpenter, "Selected Insights," in *Gay Spirit*, 152–64; and Frank B. Leib, *Friendly Competitors, Fierce Companions: Men's Ways of Relating* (Cleveland: The Pilgrim Press, 1997). On Walt Whitman, see, apart from his classic *Leaves of Grass* (New York: Quality Paperback Book Club, 1992), William Moritz, "Seven Glimpses of Walt Whitman," in *Gay Spirit*, 131–51; David S. Reynolds, *Walt Whitman's America: A Cultural Biography* (New York: Knopf, 1995); and Gary Schmidgall, *Walt Whitman: A Gay Life* (New York: Penguin Putnam Inc., 1997).

21. See Harry Hay, *Radically Gay: Gay Liberation in the Words of Its Founder*, ed. Will Roscoe (Boston: Beacon Press, 1996), and "A Separate People Whose Time Has Come," in *Gay Spirit*, 279–91; and Mark Thompson, "Harry Hay: A Voice from the Past, a Vision for the Future," in *Gay Spirit*, 182–99, and "Harry Hay: Reinventing Ourselves," in *Gay Soul* (San Francisco: HarperSanFrancisco, 1995), 78–96.

22. On the Mattachine Society, see Hay, *Radically Gay*, 35–136; and Jagose, *Queer Theory*, 22–29.

23. Thompson, "Harry Hay: A Voice from the Past," 191.

24. The Mattachine Society, structured loosely on the model of Communist cells, also borrowed the rituals of Alcoholics Anonymous for some of its meetings. In terms of its early political organizing, the men were required to wear jackets and ties and the women had to appear in dresses to project a mainstream role deserving of inclusion and acceptance by the heterosexual majority.

25. See W. Bernard Lukenbill, "Observations on the Corporate Culture of a Gay and Lesbian Congregation," *Journal for the Scientific Study of Religion* 37, no. 3 (September 1998): 440–52; and Troy D. Perry and Thomas L. P. Swicegood, *Don't Be Afraid Anymore: The Story of Reverend Troy Perry and the Metropolitan Community Churches* (New York: St. Martin's Press, 1990).

26. See John Boswell, *Christianity, Social Tolerance, and Homosexuality: Gay People in Western Europe from the Beginning of the Christian Era to the Fourteenth Century* (Chicago: University of Chicago Press, 1980); and John J. McNeill, *The Church and the Homosexual* (Kansas City: Sheed Andrews and McMeel, 1976).

27. See Troy D. Perry, *The Lord Is My Shepherd and He Knows I'm Gay: The Autobiography of the Reverend Troy D. Perry, as Told to Charles L. Lucas* (Los Angeles: Nash, 1972).

28. See the article by Michelangelo Signorile, "Church and Its Current State," *Out*, December/January 1998, 59–60.

29. Ibid., 60.

30. See, among others, Normand Bonneau, Barbara Bozak, André Guindon, and Richard Hardy, *AIDS and Faith* (Ottawa: Novalis, 1993); and Richard P. Hardy, *Knowing the God of Compassion: Spirituality and Persons Living with AIDS* (Ottawa: Novalis, 1993).

31. See Winston Leyland, ed., *Queer Dharma: Voices of Gay Buddhists* (San Francisco: Gay Sunshine Press, 1998).

32. See Susan Palmer, *AIDS as an Apocalyptic Metaphor in North America* (Toronto: University of Toronto Press, 1997), 119–45.

33. Ibid., 120.

34. Ibid.

35. Ibid., 125.

36. The reference is to Bruce Bawer's controversial book, *A Place at the Table: The Gay Individual in American Society* (New York: Poseidon Press, 1993), a typical neoconservative plea for an assimilationist strategy in gay politics.

37. John Boswell has been the real trailblazer in this regard. See *Christianity*, as well as *Same-Sex Unions in Premodern Europe* (New York: Villard Books, 1994).

38. Ibid.; McNeill, *The Church*; Peter Gomes, *The Good Book: Reading the Bible with Mind and Heart* (New York: William Morrow, 1996); Robert Goss, *Jesus Acted Up: A Gay and Lesbian Manifesto* (San Francisco: HarperCollins, 1993); and

Mark D. Jordan, *The Invention of Sodomy in Christian Theology* (Chicago: University of Chicago Press, 1997).

39. John J. McNeill, *Freedom, Glorious Freedom: The Spiritual Journey to the Fullness of Life for Gays, Lesbians, and Everybody Else* (Boston: Beacon Press, 1995), and *Taking a Chance on God: Liberating Theology for Gays, Lesbians, and Their Lovers, Families, and Friends* (Boston: Beacon Press, 1996); John E. Fortunato, *Embracing the Exile: Healing Journeys of Gay Christians* (New York: Seabury Press, 1982); Craig O'Neill and Kathleen Ritter, *Coming Out Within: Stages of Spiritual Awakening for Lesbians and Gay Men* (San Francisco: HarperSanFrancisco, 1992); and Christian de la Huerta, *Coming Out Spiritually: The Next Step* (New York: Penguin Putnam Inc., 1999).

40. Hay, *Radically Gay;* Will Roscoe, *Queer Spirits: A Gay Men's Myth Book* (Boston: Beacon Press, 1995); J. Michael Clark, especially *Defying the Darkness: Gay Theology in the Shadows* (Cleveland: The Pilgrim Press, 1997), and *Beyond Our Ghettos: Gay Theology in Ecological Perspective* (Cleveland: The Pilgrim Press, 1993); Daniel T. Spencer, *Gay and Gaia: Ethics, Ecology, and the Erotic* (Cleveland: The Pilgrim Press, 1996); and Ronald E. Long, especially "The Sacrality of Male Beauty." Another writer who should be mentioned in this listing is Mark Thompson, an anthologist of gay spirituality; see especially *Gay Spirit* and *Gay Soul*.

41. Malcolm Boyd, *Gay Priest: An Inner Journey* (New York: St. Martin's Press, 1986); John J. McNeill, *Both Feet Firmly Planted in Midair: My Spiritual Journey* (Louisville: Westminster John Knox Press, 1998); Andrew Sullivan, *Love Undetectable: Notes on Friendship, Sex, and Survival* (New York: Knopf, 1998) and "Alone Again, Naturally: The Catholic Church and the Homosexual," in *Que(e)rying Religion*, 238–50. See also the works mentioned in chapter 1, note 2 above.

42. See Bryan Wilson, *Religion in Sociological Perspective* (Oxford: Oxford University Press, 1982).

43. See Max Weber, especially *The Protestant Ethic and the Spirit of Capitalism* (New York: Charles Scribner's Sons, 1958), and *The Sociology of Religion* (Boston: Beacon Press, 1963).

44. Durkheim, *The Elementary Forms*, 22.

45. Ibid., 250; author's emphasis.

46. Frederick Bird, "The Nature and Function of Ritual Forms: A Sociological Discussion," *Studies in Religion/Sciences religieuses* (Waterloo: Wilfrid Laurier University Press) 9, no. 4 (fall 1980): 393.

47. Hans Mol, *Identity and the Sacred: A Sketch for a New Social-Scientific Theory of Religion* (Agincourt: Book Society of Canada, 1976), 233.

## 3. The Embodiment of Spirit

1. Frank Browning, *A Queer Geography: Journeys Toward a Sexual Self* (New York: Noonday Press, 1998), 137.

2. Frank Browning, "The Way of Some Flesh," in *Wrestling with the Angel*, 114. This essay contains interesting observations with respect to the similarities between spirituality and erotic experience, most notably that of a gay strip bar. See, in this regard, the comments made in chapter 5 of this book ("Holy Sex").

3. The French experience of gay politics, for example, is based not on the notion of "identity," but on the much more amorphous and ultimately conservative one of "community" or "social contract," which explains, in part, France's general resistance with respect to advocacy for gay rights.

4. See Mubarak S. Dahir, "At Play in the Fields of the Lord," *10 Percent*, January/February 1995, 52–55, 68–71. The following quotes are taken from a variety of informational broadsheets and brochures by the Brotherhood. Brother Johannes Zinzendorf, one of the two founding members, writes: "But things are different for gay men and women because, like the original Adam, we are each male and female, we can both give and receive, which means that we do not need othersa [*sic*] to achieve wholeness because we already are whole. However, we do need others with whom to express that wholeness. That is what makes gay spirituality different from, not better than, straight spirituality, just as it makes gay sex different from, not better than, straight sex. It means we contain in ourselves that primal androgeny [*sic*] and wholeness of the garden inherently, by our very nature. But it's only there as potential unless we become aware of it and make it a conscious part of our lives" (Pitman, Pa.: Harmonists of Christiansbrunn Brotherhood, electronic mail, January 18, 1999).

5. Harmonists of Christiansbrunn Brotherhood, brochure.

6. Ibid., question-and-answer information sheet.

7. Ibid., brochure.

8. Ibid.

9. See Harold Bloom, *The American Religion: The Emergence of the Post-Christian Nation* (New York: Simon & Schuster, 1992). This book provides an excellent overview of the distinctiveness of "American" religion as a form of Gnostic belief.

10. See Mark Holloway, *Heavens on Earth: Utopian Communities in America 1680–1880* (New York: Dover Publications, 1966).

11. Tim McFeeley, "Coming Out as Spiritual Revelation," *Harvard Gay & Lesbian Review* (fall 1996): 11. This viewpoint echoes the thinking of Carl Jung. See, in this regard, McNeill, *Freedom*, 181–93.

12. This debate is at the heart of the theoretical concerns of several gay writers today. The essentialist position argues that homosexuality, and therefore sexual identity, is primarily, though not exclusively, a matter of innate disposition, while the constructionist side stakes its claim for the determining influence of sociocultural factors. Most gay men, in their everyday lives, do not concern themselves unduly with this question, many of them reporting that they knew they preferred males from a very early age. Contemporary queer theory, with its

performative stance, generally tends to support the constructionist perspective. The discovery of the so-called gay gene has given credence to the essentialist point of view, while also raising serious ethical questions about future genetic manipulation and selection. See Jagose, *Queer Theory*, 8–10.

13. See Spencer, *Gay and Gaia.*

14. McNeill, *The Church*, 133; author's emphasis.

15. Thompson, *Gay Soul*, 90.

16. Spencer, *Gay and Gaia*, 118.

17. Ibid., 340.

18. Ibid., 345.

19. Ibid., 348.

20. This is the foundational element of John J. McNeill's work. See, in particular, *Taking a Chance*, part 1.

21. Ibid., 38.

22. This kind of thinking is typical of certain sectarian religious movements that are either fundamentalist or "racialist" in nature. See Palmer, *AIDS as an Apocalyptic Metaphor.*

23. The murder of Matthew Shepard, who has literally emerged as an overnight martyr in the cause of gay rights because of it, sparked a bout of collective soul-searching in the United States. In this exercise, all manner of pundits and journalists have put forward theories as to the root causes of this event. Naturally, and rather sadly, a number of them once again blame the victim, as though they were unable to look beyond a notion of ritualistic cleansing. For some rather more interesting commentary, see, among others, Tony Kushner, "Matthew's Passion," *Genre*, February 1999, 50–53, reprinted from *Nation*, November 9, 1998; Dan Savage, "The Thrill of Living Dangerously," and Elise Harris, "Writing the Book of Matthew," *Out*, March 1999, 62–65, 115–16; and Melanie Thernstrom, "The Crucifixion of Matthew Shepard," *Vanity Fair*, March 1999, 209–15, 267–75.

24. Eleanor Brown, "Queer Fear," *The Globe and Mail*, October 24, 1998.

25. St. Sebastian, a captain in the Praetorian Guard of the Roman co-emperors Diocletian and Maximian, is believed to have been martyred in the year 288. He would have been aged some thirty years. Sebastian converted secretly to Christianity, and used his position to console imprisoned Christians and convert Roman citizens to the new faith. For this reason, he was condemned to death by being shot with arrows. Tradition has it that he miraculously survived, however, and subsequently denigrated the Roman gods publicly. He was beaten to death with clubs. Sebastian's story is archetypal. Many such martyrdoms of Roman military personnel were known to have taken place.

St. Sebastian is one of the most widely painted figures in the history of art. In part this is because, except for the image of the crucified Christ, he is the only saint whose form of martyrdom made possible a legitimate visual exploration of the male body in art. In the Middle Ages, St. Sebastian was also prayed to for protection against the plague. He is often cited and used as a homoerotic icon, primarily because of the manner in which he is depicted in art.

26. See John Cloud, "Why Milk Is Still Fresh," *The Advocate*, November 10, 1998, 29–33.

27. Long, "The Sacrality of Male Beauty," 274.

## 4. Myths and Symbols of Integration and Resistance

1. See Herdt, *Same Sex*, especially chapters 3, 4, and 5; and Conner, *Blossom of Bone*. On the berdache or two-spirited tradition, see Will Roscoe, "We'wha and Klah: The American Indian Berdache as Artist and Priest," in *Que(e)rying Religion*, 89–106.

2. See the discussion of relative-deprivation theory, particularly with respect to new religious movements, in Lorne L. Dawson, *Comprehending Cults: The Sociology of New Religious Movements* (Toronto: Oxford University Press, 1998), 72–77.

3. The name of the Salesians comes from that of Saint Francis de Sales, a favorite saint of their founder, Saint John Bosco. The Italian order of priests and brothers, now found around the world, has the mission of providing education for poor boys from the working classes. John (Don) Bosco is considered one of the important personages of Italian Catholic social action in the nineteenth century.

4. Minor seminaries, which no longer exist, were high schools for boys interested in studying for the priesthood. The thinking behind them was that vocations could be developed from a young age, as early as thirteen or fourteen in most cases. They were called minor seminaries to distinguish them from the major seminary, which is where candidates for the priesthood undertook their required theological and philosophical studies prior to ordination.

5. The Congregation of the Blessed Sacrament was founded in 1856 in France by Saint Peter Julian Eymard. Its specific ministry was the propagation of the cult of the eucharist, and it was especially known for perpetual adoration of the exposed host. Its first house in North America was in Montreal in 1890, from whence it spread to the United States, with a first foundation in New York City (1900) in the parish of St. Jean Baptiste (St. John the Baptist), a predominantly French Canadian neighborhood. John the Baptist is the patron saint of French Canada.

6. Seminarians or divinity students, though exempt from military service, still had to register for the draft. The burning of draft cards was a widespread form of protest at the time of the Vietnam War. Very often, these burnings would be done collectively in the context of a march or a protest.

7. See Mircea Eliade, *Myth and Reality* (New York: Harper & Row, 1963).

8. Long, "The Sacrality of Male Beauty," 273.

9. The appearance of books, plays, and films about the distinguished Irish literary figure has been extraordinary, and Wilde himself no doubt would have relished the posthumous attention he is receiving. Among these works, the most interesting is the play by Moisés Kaufman, *Gross Indecency: The Three Trials of Oscar Wilde*, though Stephen Fry's film *Wilde* is also remarkable. One possible explanation for this interest in Wilde, quite apart from the centennial of his death in 2000, might be the general mainstreaming of gay icons as cultural artifacts, a phenomenon that is increasingly widespread in capitalist culture.

10. See Foucault, *Histoire;* and some of the essays in Martin Duberman et al., *Hidden from History: Reclaiming the Gay and Lesbian Past* (New York: NAL Books, 1989). As with Stonewall, the trial of Oscar Wilde performs an important symbolic role in gay history. Current thinking among gay historians and theorists, however, suggests that the emergence of the modern homosexual predates Wilde by one hundred years or so. See Jagose, *Queer Theory,* chapter 2.

11. See Heinz Heger, *The Men with the Pink Triangle* (London: Gay Men's Press, 1980).

12. See Foucault, *Histoire.*

13. Sullivan, *Love Undetectable,* 12–13.

14. McNeill, *Taking a Chance,* 99.

15. Sullivan, *Love Undetectable,* 24.

16. See Susan Sontag, *AIDS and Its Metaphors* (New York: Farrar, Straus & Giroux, 1988). Sontag came under attack for this book by AIDS activists, who claimed that she was merely "intellectualizing" the epidemic.

## 5. RITUALS: SEXUAL AND OTHERWISE

1. Sullivan, *Love Undetectable,* 57.

2. See the classic in the field, Arnold van Gennep, *The Rites of Passage* (Chicago: University of Chicago Press, 1960).

3. See Michelangelo Signorile, *Life Outside: The Signorile Report on Gay Men: Sex, Drugs, Muscles, and the Passages of Life* (New York: HarperCollins, 1997).

4. See note 5 below.

5. The following quotes and insights are taken from notes on a paper entitled "Circuit Parties as Spiritual Phenomenon," by Paul J. Gorrell (presented at the meeting of the American Academy of Religion, Orlando, Florida, November 21, 1998).

6. For a discussion of pilgrimages in the Christian context, see Victor Turner and Edith L. B. Turner, *Image and Pilgrimage in Christian Culture* (New York: Columbia University Press, 1978). Gay circuit parties can be analyzed as pilgrimages because there are several of them around the world at different times (hence the reason they are known as "the circuit"), and some of the same individuals frequent them assiduously. There are many analogies between the circuit party phenomenon and pilgrimage traveling.

7. See the article by Geoff Mains, "Urban Aboriginals and the Celebration of Leather Magic," in *Gay Spirit*, 111.

8. See Keith Haring, *Journals* (New York: Penguin Books, 1996). I refer here to a major Keith Haring exhibition held at the Montreal Museum of Fine Arts, November 1998 to January 1999.

9. See E. Michael Gorman, "A Special Window: An Anthropological Perspective on Spirituality in Contemporary U.S. Gay Male Culture," in *Que(e)rying Religion*, 330–37; and Philip M. Kayal, *Bearing Witness: Gay Men's Health Crisis and the Politics of AIDS* (Boulder: Westview Press, 1993).

10. It was not until 1974 that homosexuality was officially removed from the listing of mental disorders by the American Psychiatric Association.

11. Anita Bryant, a former Miss America, was a spokesperson for the Florida orange growers' industry and a born-again Christian. In the 1970s, she launched a rabid antihomosexual campaign under the banner "Save Our Children."

12. See Gary Kinsman, *The Regulation of Desire: Homo and Hetero Sexualities* (Montreal: Black Rose Books, 1996).

13. See Gorman, "A Special Window," 335–36; and Sullivan, *Love Undetectable*, 69–72.

14. Eliade's perspective, though challenged by subsequent scholars of religion, remains foundational in the field.

15. See especially Chauncey, *Gay New York*. For an interesting collection of essays on public spaces as sites of gay sexual encounter, see William L. Leap, ed., *Public Sex/Gay Space* (New York: Columbia University Press, 1999).

16. See several of the authors listed in note 12, chapter 2 above.

17. See McNeill, *Freedom*, part 2.

18. See especially Browning, *A Queer Geography*, chapter 4.

19. McNeill, *Freedom*, 62–63.

## 6. The Experience of Wholeness in Community

1. See Christopher Isherwood, *The Berlin Stories* (New York: New Directions, 1935). There are really two novels in this book: *The Last of Mr. Norris* or *Mr. Norris Changes Trains*, and *Goodbye to Berlin*.

2. As quoted in Richard Rambuss, *Closet Devotions* (Durham, N.C.: Duke University Press, 1998), 1.

3. See Antoine Faivre, *The Eternal Hermes: From Greek God to Alchemical Magus* (Grand Rapids, Mich.: Phanes Press, 1995).

4. See Thomas Mann, *Death in Venice* (New York: Random House, 1970), 88–90. It is now a well-established fact that Thomas Mann was a homosexual. In light of this fact, *Death in Venice* assumes a special significance.

5. Ibid., 90.

6. Sullivan, *Love Undetectable*, 175.

7. Ibid., 176.

## 7. Religion and Gay Culture

1. On Saints Sergius and Bacchus, see Boswell, *Same-Sex Unions*; and McNeill, *Freedom*, 86–87.

2. On the martyrs of Uganda (also known as Saint Charles Lwanga and Companions), see *Butler's Lives of the Saints (June): New Full Edition* (Collegeville, Minn.: Liturgical Press, 1998), 22–24.

3. Yukio Mishima, *Confessions of a Mask* (New York: New Directions, 1958), 38–40.

4. This book provides an eloquent and very interesting analysis of homo-eroticism as a site of transgressive religiosity. Although concerned primarily with English devotional poetry of the 1600s, the author also comments on contemporary American forms of artistic expression. It is, I believe, one of the more significant books to have appeared in the field in recent years.

5. Rambuss, *Closet Devotions*, 65.

6. Ibid., 98.

7. Ibid., 99.

8. See Leo Steinberg, *The Sexuality of Christ in Renaissance Art and in Modern Oblivion* (Chicago: University of Chicago Press, 1996).

9. Rambuss, *Closet Devotions*, 109.

10. Ibid., 135.

11. Michael Warner, "Tongues Untied: Memoirs of a Pentecostal Boyhood," in *Que(e)rying Religion*, 229–30.

12. Rambuss, *Closet Devotions*, 58.

13. See Ron Athey, "Deliverance: Introduction, Foreword, Description, and Selected Text," in *Acting on AIDS: Sex, Drugs, and Politics*, ed. Joshua Oppenheimer and Helena Reckitt (London: Serpent's Tail, 1997), 430–44.

14. See Robert C. Reinhart, *A History of Shadows* (New York: Avon Books, 1982).

15. Roy Cohn was chief legal counsel for Senator Joseph McCarthy and his infamous House Committee on Un-American Activities in the 1950s. He was also a gay man who vehemently denied it throughout his life. He died from AIDS. Tony Kushner, in his brilliant play *Angels in America*, paints Cohn as a broken symbol of self-loathing homosexuality and divine poetic justice.

16. See Jennie Hornosty, "The Contemporary Marxist-Christian Dialogue: A Study in the Political Economy of Religion with Particular Reference to Quebec" (Ph.D. diss., York University, Toronto, 1979).

17. The film is a touching portrayal of sexual variance at the heart of a macho political culture. The title refers to ice cream, which the main character uses as a metaphor for sexual difference.

# Bibliography

Athey, Ron. "Deliverance: Introduction, Foreword, Description and Selected Text." In *Acting on AIDS: Sex, Drugs, and Politics*, edited by Joshua Oppenheimer and Helena Reckitt. London: Serpent's Tail, 1997.

Baum, Gregory. *Compassion and Solidarity: The Church for Others*. Toronto: CBC Enterprises, 1987.

———. "The Homosexual Condition and Political Responsibility." In *A Challenge to Love: Gays and Lesbians in the Church*, edited by Robert Nugent. New York: Crossroad, 1983.

Bawer, Bruce. *A Place at the Table: The Gay Individual in American Society*. New York: Poseidon Press, 1993.

Bird, Frederick. "The Nature and Function of Ritual Forms: A Sociological Discussion." *Studies in Religion/Sciences religieuses* 9, no. 4 (fall 1980): 387–402.

Bloom, Harold. *The American Religion: The Emergence of the Post-Christian Nation*. New York: Simon & Schuster, 1992.

Boff, Leonardo, and Clodovis Boff. *Introducing Liberation Theology*. Maryknoll, N.Y.: Orbis Books, 1987.

Bonneau, Normand, Barbara Bozak, André Guindon, and Richard Hardy. *AIDS and Faith*. Ottawa: Novalis, 1993.

Boswell, John. *Christianity, Social Tolerance, and Homosexuality: Gay People in Western Europe from the Beginning of the Christian Era to the Fourteenth Century*. Chicago: University of Chicago Press, 1980.

———. *Same-Sex Unions in Premodern Europe*. New York: Villard Books, 1994.

Bouldrey, Brian, ed. *Wrestling with the Angel: Faith and Religion in the Lives of Gay Men*. New York: Riverhead Books, 1995.

Boyd, Malcolm. *Gay Priest: An Inner Journey.* New York: St. Martin's Press, 1986.

Brown, Eleanor. "Queer Fear." *The Globe and Mail* (Toronto), October 24, 1998.

Browning, Frank. *The Culture of Desire: Paradox and Perversity in Gay Lives Today.* New York: Random House, 1994.

———. *A Queer Geography: Journeys Toward a Sexual Self.* New York: Noonday Press, 1998.

———. "The Way of Some Flesh." In *Wrestling with the Angel: Faith and Religion in the Lives of Gay Men,* edited by Brian Bouldrey. New York: Riverhead Books, 1995.

*Butler's Lives of the Saints (June): New Full Edition.* Collegeville, Minn.: Liturgical Press, 1998.

Carmody, Denise, and John Carmody. "Homosexuality and Roman Catholicism." In *Homosexuality and World Religions,* edited by Arlene Swidler. Valley Forge, Pa.: Trinity Press International, 1993.

Carpenter, Edward. "Selected Insights." In *Gay Spirit,* edited by Mark Thompson. New York: St. Martin's Press, 1987.

Chauncey, George, Jr. *Gay New York: Gender, Urban Culture, and the Making of the Gay Male World, 1890–1940.* New York: Basic Books, 1994.

Clark, J. Michael. *Beyond Our Ghettos: Gay Theology in Ecological Perspective.* Cleveland: The Pilgrim Press, 1993.

———. *Defying the Darkness: Gay Theology in the Shadows.* Cleveland: The Pilgrim Press, 1997.

Cloud, John. "Why Milk Is Still Fresh." *The Advocate,* November 10, 1998, 29–33.

Comstock, Gary David. *Gay Theology without Apology.* Cleveland: The Pilgrim Press, 1993.

Comstock, Gary David, and Susan E. Henking, eds. *Que(e)rying Religion: A Critical Anthology.* New York: Continuum, 1997.

Conner, Randy P. *Blossom of Bone: Reclaiming the Connections between Homoeroticism and the Sacred.* San Francisco: HarperSanFrancisco, 1993.

Dahir, Mubarak S. "At Play in the Fields of the Lord." *10 Percent,* January/February 1995, 52–55, 68–71.

Daly, Mary. *Beyond God the Father: Toward a Philosophy of Women's Liberation.* Boston: Beacon Press, 1985.

———. *The Church and the Second Sex.* Boston: Beacon Press, 1985.

Dawson, Lorne L. *Comprehending Cults: The Sociology of New Religious Movements.* Toronto: Oxford University Press, 1998.

de la Huerta, Christian. *Coming Out Spiritually: The Next Step.* New York: Penguin Putnam Inc., 1999.

D'Emilio, John. *Sexual Politics, Sexual Communities: The Making of a Homosexual Minority in the United States 1940–1970.* Chicago: University of Chicago Press, 1983.

Doty, Mark. *Heaven's Coast: A Memoir.* New York: HarperCollins, 1996.

Duberman, Martin, et al., eds. *Hidden from History: Reclaiming the Gay and Lesbian Past*. New York: NAL Books, 1989.

Durkheim, Emile. *The Elementary Forms of the Religious Life*. New York: Free Press, 1915.

Eliade, Mircea. *Myth and Reality*. New York: Harper & Row, 1963.

Faivre, Antoine. *The Eternal Hermes: From Greek God to Alchemical Magus*. Grand Rapids, Mich.: Phanes Press, 1995.

Ferro, Robert. *The Family of Max Desir*. New York: New American Library, 1983.

Fortunato, John E. *Embracing the Exile: Healing Journeys of Gay Christians*. New York: Seabury Press, 1982.

Foucault, Michel. *Histoire de la sexualité 1: la volonté de savoir*. Paris: Editions Gallimard, 1976.

Gallagher, Bob, and Alexander Wilson. "Sex and the Politics of Identity: An Interview with Michel Foucault." In *Gay Spirit*, edited by Mark Thompson. New York: St. Martin's Press, 1987.

Glaser, Chris. *The Word Is Out: The Bible Reclaimed for Lesbians and Gay Men*. San Francisco: HarperSanFrancisco, 1994.

Gomes, Peter. *The Good Book: Reading the Bible with Mind and Heart*. New York: William Morrow, 1996.

Gorman, E. Michael. "A Special Window: An Anthropological Perspective on Spirituality in Contemporary U.S. Gay Male Culture." In *Que(e)rying Religion: A Critical Anthology*, edited by Gary David Comstock and Susan E. Henking. New York: Continuum, 1997.

Gorrell, Paul J. "Circuit Parties as Spiritual Phenomenon." Paper presented at the American Academy of Religion, Orlando, Florida, November 21, 1998.

Goss, Robert. *Jesus Acted Up: A Gay and Lesbian Manifesto*. San Francisco: HarperCollins, 1993.

Greenberg, David. *The Construction of Homosexuality*. Chicago: University of Chicago Press, 1988.

Gutiérrez, Gustavo. *A Theology of Liberation*. Maryknoll, N.Y.: Orbis Books, 1973.

Halperin, David. *One Hundred Years of Homosexuality and Other Essays on Greek Love*. New York: Routledge, 1990.

————. *Saint Foucault: Towards a Gay Hagiography*. New York: Oxford University Press, 1995.

Hanegraaff, Wouter J. *New Age Religion and Western Culture: Esotericism in the Mirror of Secular Thought*. Leiden: E. J. Brill, 1996.

Hardy, Richard P. *Knowing the God of Compassion: Spirituality and Persons Living with AIDS*. Ottawa: Novalis, 1993.

————. *Loving Men: Gay Partners, Spirituality, and AIDS*. New York: Continuum, 1998.

Haring, Keith. *Journals*. New York: Penguin Books, 1996.

Harmonists of Christiansbrunn Brotherhood. Pitman, Pa.: sundry informational material.

Harris, Elise. "Writing the Book of Matthew." *Out*, March 1999, 62–65, 115–16.

Hay, Harry. *Radically Gay: Gay Liberation in the Words of Its Founder*, ed. Will Roscoe. Boston: Beacon Press, 1996.

———. "A Separate People Whose Time Has Come." In *Gay Spirit*, edited by Mark Thompson. New York: St. Martin's Press, 1987.

Heger, Heinz. *The Men with the Pink Triangle*. London: Gay Men's Press, 1980.

Herdt, Gilbert. *Same Sex, Different Cultures: Exploring Gay and Lesbian Lives*. Boulder, Colo.: Westview Press, 1997.

Holleran, Andrew. *Dancer from the Dance*. New York: William Morrow, 1978.

Holloway, Mark. *Heavens on Earth: Utopian Communities in America 1680–1880*. New York: Dover Publications, 1996.

Hornosty, Jennie. "The Contemporary Marxist-Christian Dialogue: A Study in the Political Economy of Religion with Particular Reference to Quebec." Ph.D. diss., York University (Toronto), 1979.

Isherwood, Christopher. *The Berlin Stories*. New York: New Directions, 1935.

———. *A Single Man*. New York: Avon Books, 1964.

Jagose, Annamarie. *Queer Theory: An Introduction*. New York: New York University Press, 1996.

James, William Clossen. *Locations of the Sacred: Essays on Religion, Literature, and Canadian Culture*. Waterloo, Ont.: Wilfrid Laurier University Press, 1998.

Jay, Karla, and Allen Young, eds. *Out of the Closets: Voices of Gay Liberation*. New York: Pyramid Books, 1974.

Jordan, Mark D. *The Invention of Sodomy in Christian Theology*. Chicago: University of Chicago Press, 1997.

Kayal, Philip M. *Bearing Witness: Gay Men's Health Crisis and the Politics of AIDS*. Boulder, Colo.: Westview Press, 1993.

Kinsman, Gary. *The Regulation of Desire: Homo and Hetero Sexualities*. Montreal: Black Rose Books, 1996.

Kramer, Larry. *Faggots*. New York: Warner, 1978.

———. "Matthew's Passion." *Genre*, February 1999, 50–53.

Leap, William L., ed. *Public Sex/Gay Space*. New York: Columbia University Press, 1999.

Leavitt, David. *Family Dancing*. New York: Warner, 1983.

Leib, Frank B. *Friendly Competitors, Fierce Companions: Men's Ways of Relating*. Cleveland: The Pilgrim Press, 1997.

Leyland, Winston, ed. *Queer Dharma: Voices of Gay Buddhists*. San Francisco: Gay Sunshine Press, 1998.

Long, Ronald E. "The Sacrality of Male Beauty and Homosex: A Neglected Factor in the Understanding of Contemporary Gay Reality." In *Que(e)rying Religion: A Critical Anthology*, edited by Gary David Comstock and Susan E. Henking. New York: Continuum, 1997.

Lukenbill, W. Bernard. "Observations on the Corporate Culture of a Gay and Lesbian Congregation." *Journal for the Scientific Study of Religion* 37, no. 3 (September 1998): 440–52.

Mains, Geoff. "Urban Aboriginals and the Celebration of Leather Magic." In *Gay Spirit*, edited by Mark Thompson. New York: St. Martin's Press, 1987.

Mann, Thomas. *Death in Venice*. New York: Random House, 1970.

Marx, Karl. *On Religion*. Ed. Saul K. Padover. New York: McGraw-Hill, 1974.

McFeeley, Tim. "Coming Out as Spiritual Revelation." *Harvard Gay & Lesbian Review* 3, no. 4 (fall 1996): 9–11.

McNeill, John J. *Both Feet Firmly Planted in Midair: My Spiritual Journey*. Louisville, Ky.: Westminster John Knox Press, 1998.

———. *The Church and the Homosexual*. Kansas City: Sheed Andrews and McMeel, 1976.

———. *Freedom, Glorious Freedom: The Spiritual Journey to the Fullness of Life for Gays, Lesbians, and Everybody Else*. Boston: Beacon Press, 1995.

———. *Taking a Chance on God: Liberating Theology for Gays, Lesbians, and Their Lovers, Families, and Friends*. Boston: Beacon Press, 1996.

Mishima, Yukio. *Confessions of a Mask*. New York: New Directions, 1958.

Mol, Hans. *Identity and the Sacred: A Sketch for a New Social-Scientific Theory of Religion*. Agincourt, Ont.: Book Society of Canada, 1976.

Moritz, William. "Seven Glimpses of Walt Whitman." In *Gay Spirit*, edited by Mark Thompson. New York: St. Martin's Press, 1987.

*Mother Jones*, November/December 1997.

Murphy, Timothy F., and Suzanne Poirier, eds. *Writing AIDS: Gay Literature, Language, and Analysis*. New York: Columbia University Press, 1993.

Murray, Stephen O., and Will Roscoe. *Islamic Homosexualities: Culture, History, and Literature*. New York: New York University Press, 1997.

Northup, Lesley A. *Ritualizing Women*. Cleveland: The Pilgrim Press, 1997.

Nugent, Robert, ed. *A Challenge to Love: Gays and Lesbians in the Church*. New York: Crossroad, 1983.

Ochs, Carol. *Behind the Sex of God*. Boston: Beacon Press, 1977.

O'Neill, Craig, and Kathleen Ritter. *Coming Out Within: Stages of Spiritual Awakening for Lesbians and Gay Men*. San Francisco: HarperSanFrancisco, 1992.

Oppenheimer, Joshua, and Helena Reckitt, eds. *Acting on AIDS: Sex, Drugs, and Politics*. London: Serpent's Tail, 1997.

Palmer, Susan. *AIDS as an Apocalyptic Metaphor in North America*. Toronto: University of Toronto Press, 1997.

Perry, Troy D., and Thomas L. P. Swicegood. *Don't Be Afraid Anymore: The Story of Reverend Troy Perry and the Metropolitan Community Churches*. New York: St. Martin's Press, 1990.

———. *The Lord Is My Shepherd and He Knows I'm Gay: The Autobiography of the Reverend Troy D. Perry, as Told to Charles L. Lucas*. Los Angeles: Nash, 1972.

Rambuss, Richard. *Closet Devotions*. Durham, N.C.: Duke University Press, 1998.

Reinhart, Robert C. *A History of Shadows*. New York: Avon Books, 1982.

Reynolds, David S. *Walt Whitman's America: A Cultural Biography*. New York: Knopf, 1995.

Roscoe, Will. *Queer Spirits: A Gay Men's Myth Book*. Boston: Beacon Press, 1995.

———. "We'wha and Klah: The American Indian Berdache as Artist and Priest." In *Que(e)rying Religion: A Critical Anthology*, edited by Gary David Comstock and Susan E. Henking. New York: Continuum, 1997.

Ruether, Rosemary Radford. *Women-Church: Theology and Practice*. San Francisco: Harper & Row, 1985.

Savage, Dan. "The Thrill of Living Dangerously." *Out*, March 1999, 62–65, 115–16.

Schmidgall, Gary. *Walt Whitman: A Gay Life*. New York: Penguin Putnam Inc., 1997.

Shallenberger, David. *Reclaiming the Spirit: Gay Men and Lesbians Come to Terms with Religion*. New Brunswick, N.J.: Rutgers University Press, 1998.

Signorile, Michelangelo. "Church and Its Current State." *Out*, December/January 1998, 59–60.

———. *Life Outside: The Signorile Report on Gay Men: Sex, Drugs, Muscles, and the Passages of Life*. New York: HarperCollins, 1997.

Sontag, Susan. *AIDS and Its Metaphors*. New York: Farrar, Straus & Giroux, 1988.

Spencer, Daniel T. *Gay and Gaia: Ethics, Ecology, and the Erotic*. Cleveland: The Pilgrim Press, 1996.

Steinberg, Leo. *The Sexuality of Christ in Renaissance Art and in Modern Oblivion*. Chicago: University of Chicago Press, 1996.

Stuart, Elizabeth, et al. *Religion Is a Queer Thing: A Guide to the Christian Faith for Lesbian, Gay, Bisexual, and Transgendered People*. Cleveland: The Pilgrim Press, 1997.

Sullivan, Andrew. "Alone Again, Naturally: The Catholic Church and the Homosexual." In *Que(e)rying Religion: A Critical Anthology*, edited by Gary David Comstock and Susan E. Henking. New York: Continuum, 1997.

———. *Love Undetectable: Notes on Friendship, Sex, and Survival*. New York: Knopf, 1998.

Sweasey, Peter. *From Queer to Eternity: Spirituality in the Lives of Lesbians, Gay, and Bisexual People*. London: Cassell, 1997.

Swidler, Arlene, ed. *Homosexuality and World Religions*. Valley Forge, Pa.: Trinity Press International, 1993.

Thernstrom, Melanie. "The Crucifixion of Matthew Shepard." *Vanity Fair*, March 1999, 209–15, 267–75.

Thompson, Mark. *Gay Soul*. San Francisco: HarperSanFrancisco, 1995.

———. *Gay Spirit: Myth and Meaning.* New York: St. Martin's Press, 1987.

———. "Harry Hay: A Voice from the Past, a Vision for the Future." In *Gay Spirit*, edited by Mark Thompson. New York: St. Martin's Press, 1987.

———. "Harry Hay: Reinventing Ourselves." In *Gay Soul*, edited by Mark Thompson. San Francisco: HarperSanFrancisco, 1995.

Turner, Victor, and Edith L. B. Turner. *Image and Pilgrimage in Christian Culture.* New York: Columbia University Press, 1978.

van Gennep, Arnold. *The Rites of Passage.* Chicago: University of Chicago Press, 1960.

Warner, Michael. "Tongues Untied: Memoirs of a Pentecostal Boyhood." In *Que(e)rying Religion: A Critical Anthology*, edited by Gary David Comstock and Susan E. Henking. New York: Continuum, 1997.

———, ed. *Fear of a Queer Planet: Queer Politics and Social Theory.* Minneapolis: University of Minnesota Press, 1993.

Warren, Patricia Nell. *The Front Runner.* New York: William Morrow, 1974.

Waugh, Thomas. *Hard to Imagine: Gay Male Eroticism in Photography and Film from Their Beginnings to Stonewall.* New York: Columbia University Press, 1996.

Weber, Max. *The Protestant Ethic and the Spirit of Capitalism.* New York: Charles Scribner's Sons, 1958.

———. *The Sociology of Religion.* Boston: Beacon Press, 1963.

Weeks, Jeffrey. *Coming Out: Homosexual Politics in Britain from the Nineteenth Century to the Present.* London: Quartet Books, 1977.

White, Edmund. *The Beautiful Room Is Empty.* New York: Random House, 1988.

———. *A Boy's Own Story.* New York: New American Library, 1982.

White, Edmund, and Adam Mars-Jones. *The Darker Proof: Stories from a Crisis.* New York: New American Library, 1988.

Whitman, Walt. *Leaves of Grass.* New York: Quality Paperback Book Club, 1992.

Wilson, Bryan. *Religion in Sociological Perspective.* Oxford: Oxford University Press, 1982.

Wilson, Nancy. "Fear of Faith." *Harvard Gay & Lesbian Review* (fall 1996): 18–19.

Yip, Andrew K. T. *Gay Male Christian Couples: Life Stories.* Westport, Conn.: Praeger, 1997.

Zinzendorf, Brother Johannes. "Gay Spirituality: Column." Pitman, Pa.: The Hermitage, electronic mail, January 18, 1999.

# Index